True Horse & Pony Stories

Other books by Diana Pullein-Thompson in Armada

Ponies in the Valley
Horses at Home
I Wanted a Pony
Janet Must Ride
A Pony for Sale
A Pony to School

by Christine Pullein-Thompson

Good Riding
Riding for Fun

by Charlotte Popescu

Pony Care from A–Z
Armada Horse & Pony Quiz Books Nos. 1 & 2

True Horse & Pony Stories

Compiled by
Diana Pullein-Thompson

True Horse & Pony Stories
was first published in Armada in 1976 by
William Collins Sons & Co. Ltd.,
14 St James's Place, London SW1A 1PF

Printed in Great Britain by
Love & Malcomson Ltd., Brighton Road,
Redhill, Surrey.

CONTENTS

ACKNOWLEDGEMENTS

The editor would like to thank the following for permission to use material in this book:

Josephine Pullein-Thompson for 'A Crazy Gallop', © Josephine Pullein-Thompson 1976; Stella Walker, and The Hamlyn Group, for 'Wellington's War Horse', originally published in her book, HORSES OF RENOWN; Joan Selby Lowndes for 'Little Billy The Circus Horse', © Joan Selby Lowndes 1976; Cynthia Muir for her story 'The Pony Who Thought She Was A Dog'; Dorothea Cannan for 'Horses of Long Ago', © Dorothea Cannan 1976; Barbara Woodhouse, and Euro-Features Ltd., for 'The Mare with the Bad White Face' originally published in her book, TALKING TO ANIMALS, by Souvenir Press Ltd., Eric Squires, and David & Charles Publishers, for 'Jimmy and Tiggy' originally published in his book, PIT PONY HEROES; James Herriot, and David Higham Associates Ltd., for 'An Old-Fashioned Cure' originally published in his book, IT SHOULDN'T HAPPEN TO A VET, by Michael Joseph Publishers; Christine Pullein-Thompson for 'Rescue at Tea-time', © Christine Pullein-Thompson 1976; Michael Hardcastle for 'Red Rum', © Michael Hardcastle 1976; Monica Dickens, and William Heinemann Ltd., for 'A Ride by the Sea' originally published in her book, TALKING OF HORSES.

'Shandy', 'Lost on the Moors' and 'Tarragona' are all © Diana Pullein-Thompson 1976.

Thanks are also due for the photographs to:
The Press Association for Red Rum; The Duke of Wellington's Collection at Stratfield Saye House for Haydon's Copenhagen; The National Coal Board for the pit ponies; Cynthia Muir for Jan the Shetland Pony, Monica Dickens for herself and John; Christine Pullein-Thompson for herself on Lorraine, and Dorothea Cannan for the pony in Oxford.

THE CRAZY GALLOP

by Josephine Pullein-Thompson

It was a misty November day and we were hunting. We had just drawn a covert blank and now we were hacking across the land of a horsy farmer who kept every hedge on his farm neat and jumpable and wire-free.

The Woodland was a small pack. The only professional was the kennel-huntsman. My sisters and I helped him with the hound exercise and every Saturday we provided two whippers-in.

This week Diana on grey Favorita and Christine on grey Lorraine were the whips, while I, riding a dark bay thoroughbred mare called Symphony, relaxed as a member of the field.

Being identical twins, Diana and Christine were the same size and shape, and dressed alike in black caps, coats and boots and cream breeches and both riding grey mares, it was impossible for most people to tell them apart unless they knew that Christine was acting as first whipper-in, Diana as second.

The first whip has much the best time, leading the pack along the roads, going on ahead to mark points, galloping across country with the huntsman when hounds find. The poor old second whip's job is always to hang back, sending on the lagging hounds, counting them whenever the opportunity occurs. He spends his time cracking his whip and shouting "Forrad on", and "'Ike on to him", in some dark, dank wood and listening hopefully for the huntsman to blow the two short toots on his horn that mean "All on". And at the end of the day he stays out looking for lost hounds. We took the two jobs in turn.

Christine's Lorraine was a fairly new acquisition. She was a good jumper, a hard, lean fifteen-two. We'd bought her from some people who wanted to show-jump her and who seemed to have upset her thoroughly with some cruel method aimed at producing clear rounds. When we had tried her she had been a sweating, martingaled-down maniac covered in warts, but we'd liked her and, since none of the warts was in a position to be rubbed by saddle, bridle or girth, we'd taken a chance on getting rid of them and had bought her. Then an extraordinary thing happened, for after we had had her for a few weeks we suddenly noticed that every wart had vanished, never to come back. I suppose there must have been a psychological cause—perhaps she had been desperately worried by her inability to clear the show jumps, and when this was removed, she became relaxed and happy and recovered.

The members of the field were chattering happily as they rode towards the new covert, the farmer had reported that he believed an old dog fox to be lying there, and as we approached Christine was sent into action. She'd obviously been told to gallop on to the far side of the covert and let the huntsman know if a fox went away; we whips carried whistles for this purpose so that the huntsman could tell our signals from the hollers of the bystanders and the field.

Christine set off. In full view of us all she took a big hedge with graceful ease—then something seemed to go wrong. Lorraine began to buck and kick, which was unusual for her. Then she seemed to go absolutely frantic, bucking, kicking and plunging in mad circles as though trying to dislodge some stinging insect, some biting animal. We hurried towards her and saw, looking over the hedge, that her girth had slipped. It had slipped back over her not very well-sprung ribs and was dangling round her belly, against her stifles, playing the part of a tickling strap on a rodeo horse and driving her distracted.

I put Symphony at the hedge and jumped into the same field. Then I tried to approach. If I could grab the reins I might be able to hang on and keep her still long enough for Christine to unbuckle the girth. But Lorraine was crazy with fear. Lashing out in all directions, swinging round and round in her terror, quite oblivious of voice or rein, she struggled to escape from the horror encircling her belly.

Symphony, infected by her terror, refused to go near. I tried to force her, but she stood trembling, ears pricked, eyes bulging; I and my aids were ignored.

Suddenly Lorraine tried a new tactic, and flung herself backwards into the hedge. Half falling as she lost her footing in the ditch, she lurched and struggled.

"Get off!" we were all shouting at Christine. "Jump for it." I had visions of my sister crushed beneath the maddened horse while I watched helplessly. Christine jumped free. As she did so the saddle, which had been held in position by her weight and Lorraine's prominent wither, slipped, and as Lorraine struggled out of the ditch we saw that the girth was over her loins, the saddle dangling under her belly, the heavy stirrup irons swinging backwards and forwards, cracking against her hind legs.

She began to buck again. Christine tried to take the reins, but it was impossible to get near, the wildly lashing hoofs were never still for a second. She was a mad thing, our soothing cries had no effect at all, she was alone with her terror and no longer saw us as people who could help.

She bucked and bucked and then suddenly, as though coming to a decision, as though she had decided to try flight, she turned and set off at a gallop. Across the fields she went, taking the hedges in her stride, flying over them despite the dangling saddle, the stirrup irons beating her hind legs

I could see that she was purposeful now. She meant to gallop and gallop until this terrible thing, this incubus, fell from her. Symphony and I followed, taking the hedges in her wake, hoping to catch her when something too large to jump barred her way. But nothing seemed too large. We followed her over some enormous hedges. She was heading for the farmyard.

I could see a group of foot followers coming towards us and one turned and ran back to close the yard gate. It was a solid, daunting, outsizc five-barred gate, not the sort you expect a hunter to jump. But Lorraine had decided that only flight could free her. She steadied her gallop and took the gate easily, then she vanished among the farm buildings. Someone swung it open for me. "Anyone hurt?" they asked as I clattered through. "No," I shouted back, trotting noisily across the concrete and past the buildings. Surely the other great gate into the road would have stopped Lorraine?

It was closed, a good five feet high, the take-off concrete, the landing gravel. But on the other side the ducks were quacking nervously, children were pointing, not right, in the direction of home, but left, down the road towards the river. A road that led to one of the many pairs of small towns and villages grouped along the river's banks.

I took Symphony on the grass verge and cantered in pursuit. Lorraine hadn't used the verge, I could tell by the long, white slip marks that her shod hoofs had scored on the road. We cantered along the edge of the green and came to a small crossroads where I slowed down looking for indications of which way she had taken, then a motorist coming up the main road waved and pointed behind him. Well, that was one car she hadn't collided with, I thought, as we clattered past the old forge, but, if she didn't crash into a car or lorry head-on, she would certainly fall and break her knees. I tried to steel myself against the horror of a mangled grey figure dripping blood.

Symphony seemed to feel the same sense of urgency as I did. She kept up a steady canter along the grit-softened edge of the road without needing any encouragement from me. But the hill lay ahead. It was well-known locally. Steep with a slippery surface, narrow with high banks, perilous to cars in time of sudden snow, a nightmare to inexperienced drivers towing trailers. If Lorraine went down at a flat-out gallop she was bound to fall. In my imagination I saw the broken knees again, bloody wounds full of grit, the precious joint oil escaping. She'd be lame for life if that happened.

We came to the brink of the hill and I slowed to a trot, there was no point in risking two pairs of broken knees. Nimble, well-balanced, dressage schooled, Symphony was a good horse for the job and we both concentrated grimly on keeping her on her feet. At first high hedge-topped banks kept us firmly on the narrow road, then a beech copse offered a leafy verge, we crossed over and cantered rustling through the newly fallen leaves.

The hill grew steeper. Lorraine hadn't tried to find a safer surface, she'd galloped straight down the centre of the road. I could tell by the white marks cut by her shoes, which were longer now as she slipped and slithered down the hill in long skids. A motor cyclist going down roared past me, the drivers of cars coming up waved me on, shouted incomprehensible remarks. Luckily they had to come slowly, in low gear. Perhaps that was giving them time to stop or swerve if they met her head on.

Symphony's clipped, mouse-brown neck was sweating, the beech leaves came to an end and we were on the road again. I decided to cross over and take the precipitous path along the bank, some ten or twelve feet above the road. We could canter down that.

We climbed up and cantered on. Still no sign of Lorraine, only the skid marks. The bank path ended. The high walls of cottages and gardens enclosed us, hoofbeats echoed between them. There were ways off the road, drives and lanes, but the skid marks led straight on. Another road branched off, but beyond it, outside the village shop, an excited group waved and called to me.

"He's gone on, towards the toll-bridge—not half a minute since. Anyone hurt?"

The toll bridge over the river, I thought, as Symphony's hoofs hammered through the village street. Would the keeper hear her coming and shut the gate? It was really high—six or seven feet. A real Dick Turpin toll gate, the sort he and Bess had jumped on the ride to York. I began to feel more cheerful, I expected to see an exhausted grey, sides heaving, sweat dripping, but when I came round the corner I saw that the gate was open and the keeper stood outside his small white house, gazing across the bridge.

"Went through at full gallop," he shouted. "I tried to stop him, but he wasn't having any. Go on, go on." He waved me through without demanding his fee.

Symphony's hoofs echoed hollowly over the water.

My expectation of disaster grew and grew. Lorraine was going to gallop into the small town's busy shopping street, it was a major road too, a lorry and bus route. All day long a constant stream of traffic used it. There was a halt sign, but Lorraine wouldn't halt, she would burst unexpectedly into the traffic and collide with whatever happened to be passing. She would be killed or at least horribly injured and the unsuspecting people in the cars and buses, the passers-by could all be hurt too. In my mind's eye I saw the pile-up, the broken-legged horse lying with pain-grazed eyes among the buckled cars.

Symphony was trembling as we trotted under the railway bridge, a small brick tunnel hooped across the road, and then we were in the town: boutique, off-licence, chemist, hotel, another wine merchant, a grocer, W. H. Smith. But the traffic still flowed, passing in an unending procession along the unflurried street. There was no sign of Lorraine.

But, as Symphony and I stood at the halt sign, passers-by gathered round us.

"She went straight across." They pointed. "Through the little opening between Smith's and the wine shop."

"A furniture van just missed her, I don't know how the driver did it," a man told me. "A miracle the horse wasn't killed."

"Could have been a nasty accident," they agreed, shaking their heads.

A gap came in the traffic, Symphony and I trotted briskly across and took the gravelled lane that led between two rows of cottages. Here all was quiet, but further up I could see people standing at their garden gates.

A helmeted young man wheeling a motor cycle came towards me. "She's stopped," he said. "She's just up there on the footpath."

As I thanked him I realised that he was the motor cyclist who had passed me on the hill, he must have joined in the chase.

I rode to the end of the lane. From it a yard-wide footpath led on between back gardens and a field and on it stood Lorraine. Head hanging, sides heaving, her grey coat streaked with grimy sweat; all the fight seemed to have gone out of her, she stood utterly dejected, resigned to the saddle which still dangled under her belly.

I dismounted and talked to her as I approached. I looked first at her knees, they were untouched. Then at the trickles of blood down her hindlegs. They didn't seem serious, just blood from the cuts and bruises caused by the banging stirrup irons.

I unbuckled the girth and righted the saddle. The tree seemed unbroken and the saddle undamaged except for a few scrapes and scratches. I manoeuvred the two horses up the narrow path and into the lane.

"There's blood on her legs and on the saddle," a bystander pointed out.

"Was her rider hurt?" asked another.

I explained that my sister had been able to jump clear, thanked the motor cyclist again and set off down the lane leading the two horses. Lorraine seemed sound at the walk, though she was obviously exhausted, so I climbed back on Symphony and started the journey to the village where hounds had met.

All the way back people called out to me, "You got him then!"

"Is she all right?"

"Anyone hurt?"

Little boys pointed ghoulishly to the saddle. "Look at that blood!" they said.

Christine and all the members of the first were very relieved to hear that Lorraine was still in one piece when, having sent her home by box, I at last caught up with them. But I don't think any of them realised what a fright I had had.

Lorraine was stiff and sore for a few days, then she completely recovered and seemed to have forgotten all about her horrible experience.

My memory was longer, and since that day I have been a great advocate of breastplates, especially for horses with powerful shoulders and not very well-sprung ribs.

WELLINGTON'S WAR HORSE

by Stella Walker
(From "Horses of Renown")

Copenhagen's endurance was renowned. On the day before the Battle of Waterloo, Wellington rode him almost sixty miles visiting the Prussian troops' headquarters and attending conferences with his generals.

The Duke wrote: "On June 17th before 10 o'clock I got on Copenhagen's back—so much to do that neither he nor I were still for many minutes together. I never drew bit and he never had a morsel in his mouth till 8 p.m. The poor beast I myself saw stabled in the village of Waterloo."

Seven hours later, at three o'clock in the morning, Wellington rose and wrote important letters. As soon as it was light he mounted Copenhagen and rode him throughout the entire battle, a period in all of over seventeen hours. Unafraid of cannon shots, rainstorms and the terrible cavalry charges of General Ney, Wellington on Copenhagen calmly directed operations, galloping from one viewpoint to another to see how the battle was going. He launched the Household Cavalry against the French with the words, "Now, gentlemen, for the honour of the Household Cavalry!" When the enemy captured La Haye Sainte, Wellington, still riding Copenhagen, took command of the Brunswickers and saved the day. He seemed to be everywhere on the gallant chestnut stallion, oblivious of danger. The final phase of the battle lasted from seven-thirty in the evening until it was dark. At nine, Wellington rode forward to greet Blucher, who had commanded the Prussian troops, on the Brussels road between Rossomme and La Bella Alliance.

Although the two commanders greeted each other cheerfully in this hour of victory, Wellington's heart was heavy for the British losses had been immense. Wearily he returned on Copenhagen to the village of Waterloo across the battlefield, where 45,000 dead and wounded lay in an area of three square miles. As Wellington and the charger picked their way along the muddy road in bright moonlight, wounded men recognised the pair and roused themselves from their pain and delirium to cheer as they passed. But the Duke was sunk in deep depression, worn out by sheer physical fatigue and devastated with grief at the appalling losses his victory had brought about. At eleven he reached his quarters, dismounted and gave Copenhagen a friendly pat on his rump, whereupon the chestnut, perhaps feeling that the hour of triumph merited some display of spirit, lashed out and only by inches missed killing his master.

The next day, when the Duke and Copenhagen were in Brussels, the horse once more kicked up his heels as his rider dismounted and this time he broke loose and galloped half through the city before he was recaptured.

After the Battle of Waterloo, Copenhagen retired to the Duke's estate, Strathfield Saye. He was ridden here by the Duke and his friends and used for breeding. He wasn't pure thoroughbred and so was not able to be entered in the General Stud Book, but his dam, Lady Catherine, had been a fine charger, carrying General Grosvenor at the Siege of Copenhagen and his sire, Meteor, had been second in the 1786 Derby and was the son of the famous racehorse Eclipse. Wellington had bought Copenhagen from Sir Charles Stewart in Spain in 1812, where he had served as a charger, and rode him throughout the Peninsular Campaign.

For the last ten years of his life, Copenhagen, accidentally blinded in one eye, was not ridden. The Duke's devotion to the horse never lessened and when Copenhagen died in 1836 he was buried with military honours at Strathfield Saye. Wellington gave much thought to the wording of the headstone. He sent two suggestions to his friend, Lady Dorothy Neville, asking which she thought best.

> "Here, full of honour and great memories,
> Wellington's war-horse Copenhagen lies.
> Spare empty praise to one so tried and true,
> These words suffice: Peace—Victory—Waterloo!"

or:

"God's humble instrument, though coarser clay,
Should have his meed on that heroic day."

Lady Neville chose the first of the two, at which the Duke wrote back to say she was no judge of epitaphs. He had chosen the second, which had been written by himself, the first having been composed by the Reverend Mr. Haweis.

The epitaph which eventually appeared on the headstone read:

Here lies
COPENHAGEN,
The charger ridden by the Duke of Wellington
The entire day at the Battle of Waterloo.
Born 1808. Died 1836.
God's humbler instrument, though meaner clay,
Should share the glory of that glorious day.

Years later, in extreme old age, the Duke would still talk of his famous horse and relate endless stories of his fire and energy. He is recorded as saying: "There may be faster, no doubt many handsomer, but for bottom and endurance I never saw his fellow."

In London, opposite Apsley House at Hyde Park Corner, there is a fine bronze statue by Sir Joseph Edgar Boehm of Wellington on Copenhagen. The most successful portrait is by James Ward, which was painted as a companion picture to Napoleon on Marengo.

LITTLE BILLY THE CIRCUS HORSE

by Joan Selby Lowndes

It was a bright, blustery spring day and the Smithfield horse market was crowded.

"Want to buy a good 'orse?" A sharp-eyed dealer called out to a tall, powerfully-built young man who was elbowing his way through the throng.

"What've you got?" Philip Astley's voice boomed through the racket of the market. Keeping a firm hold on the bag of money in his coat pocket, he made his way over to a bunch of horses tied up in a corner.

To Philip Astley's practised eye this was the usual job-lot of dealer's animals: worn-out old horses; bewildered youngsters, still unbroken; and working horses of all shapes and sizes—for this was the year 1766, when horses were still the only form of transport.

"What about that there animal?" Astley pointed suddenly to a small brown horse.

"That one?" The dealer was surprised for this was a nondescript animal that most people wouldn't look at twice. However, he quickly untied him and turned him round.

"It's a good young horse, sir!" He started on his selling routine. "Sound in wind and limb . . ."

But Astley wasn't listening. He didn't need anyone to tell him about a horse. He was staring thoughtfully at the young animal. It was neither showy nor handsome, but it looked strong and sturdy, and it had a bold, bright eye. There was something about that cheeky look which took Astley's fancy.

The bargaining began.

It ended when Astley pulled the bag of coins out of his pocket and carefully counted five gold sovereigns into the dealer's grimy hand.

Neither of them could know then that for five pounds he had just bought the horse that was to lay the foundations of his fortune and make the name of Astley famous in circus history.

Little Billy was put into stables at Islington, close to Astley's lodgings, and his training began.

Philip Astley was a born horseman, and six years in the cavalry had given him the knowledge and experience he needed to train and handle horses. He was an ambitious man, and when he discovered that there was fame and fortune to be won by giving displays of horsemanship, he had left the army to try his luck.

His first piece of luck had been the gift of a handsome white horse, presented to him by his commanding officer. His second piece of luck was Little Billy.

Astley soon discovered that his small brown horse was a star pupil. Bold, good-tempered, and quick to learn, Billy soon graduated from his basic training to dressage and high school work. All through the long summer months of 1767 the patient schooling went on. During this time Astley studied the competition facing them. Displays of trick-riding were a novelty. Nearby, at *"The Three Hats"* in Islington, a Mr. Price was winning applause and money for galloping round a track standing upright on the saddle. In a field not far away, a rival, Mr. Sampson, went one better by standing on his head on the saddle of a galloping horse. Astley promptly taught himself to do both tricks. Then he heard of an entirely new type of entertainment.

At the Belvedere Tea Gardens in Pentonville, Mr. Zucker presented "A Little Learned Horse" that was attracting the crowds. Astley went to see the show, and found himself watching a horse which had been trained to perform on its own.

The Little Learned Horse answered questions by nodding or shaking his head. He could add up by striking the ground with his foreleg. He walked about carrying a handkerchief in his mouth. He even lay down and got up to a word of command.

This was something quite new, and Astley, who was always quick to make use of other people's ideas, decided to teach Billy to do the same tricks.

He set to work and found, to his delight, that Billy was a born actor.

"I shall present him as the Little Military Learned Horse," Astley declared. But the question was—where?

He began looking round for a show-ground where he would be free of rivals.

He found it on the south bank of the river—a derelict field called Halfpenny Hatch. This was an unfashionable part of London. There were no tea gardens to attract the public, but the field lay alongside the busy turnpike road between Blackfriars Bridge and Westminster. Astley was gambling on his own ability to pull in the public. He hired it for the summer and moved in.

"Walk up! Walk up! Ladies and gentlemen . . ." A booming voice echoing over Westminster Bridge made passers-by turn and stare at the spectacular sight of ex-Sergeant Major Astley, in full military uniform, astride his showy white horse. Blowing a trumpet and distributing handbills, he shouted himself hoarse announcing: "Amazing exhibitions of horsemanship to be given daily! First performance to take place on the fourth of April. Doors opening at four p.m."

But how many would come?

Inside the show-ground, tension grew as Astley and his wife dragged the wooden benches into place round the roped-off riding arena. They kept an anxious eye on the treacherous, cloud-filled April sky. A shower of rain could wash out all their hopes.

"Sir! Sir!" The odd-job boy, shrill with excitement, came scampering across the grass. "There's people gathering outside!"

Astley hurried away to the rickety shed that served as a stable to have a last look at his horses. The three of them stood ready, saddled and bridled, and the sight of their shining coats and hard muscles gave him a lift of pride. Every penny of his savings had gone into preparing for this moment.

Little Billy turned his head and whickered softly at the sight of his master. Astley went to give his favourite a last pat. He knew that, whatever else happened, his horses wouldn't let him down.

A church clock struck four, and he strode away to unbar the gates.

"This way, ladies and gentlemen!" Astley bawled. "One shilling for a seat, sixpence to stand."

A steady trickle of people came through and, by five o'clock, the ground had filled with a noisy, excited crowd. Up on a stand perched the odd-job boy with a drum, waiting.

Astley gave the signal to begin. There was a roll on the drum. The buzz of voices died away to a breathless hush as all eyes turned to watch a tall figure on a prancing white horse entering the arena.

Philip Astley, the showman, faced his first audience.

The show began with the simplest tricks, copied from Price and Sampson, Astley galloped his horse round the arena standing on the saddle, first on one leg, and then facing backwards. Finally he stood on his head. There was a gasp from the crowd as, still upside down, he pulled out a pistol. There was a roar and a spurt of flame. The next moment Astley was on his feet again, the smoking pistol still in his hand. Enthusiastic applause broke out. The crowd were warming to him.

Astley brought in his second horse, and rode the pair at a gallop round the arena, one foot on each, ending with a spectacular jump over a pole. The crowd were thrilled.

They were now to see the highlight of the show.

"Ladies and gentlemen!" the sergeant major voice boomed out, "I beg leave to introduce, for your entertainment, The Little Military Learned Horse!"

There was a pause. The crowd gaped. Into the arena walked a small brown horse. He stood quietly at his master's side.

"This horse will, in a manner most entertaining, appear dead," Astley yelled.

There was a murmur from the crowd, as Billy, obeying the secret signal, lay down at Astley's feet, rolled over on his side and stretched his head out on the ground.

"My horse lies dead, apparent at your sight, but I'm the man can set the thing to right," bawled Astley the poet, who had found it much harder to make up the rhyme than to train Billy.

"That he is dead is quite beyond dispute . . ." Astley picked up a relaxed foreleg and let it drop in the most realistic manner. The crowd began to be anxious.

"Speak when you please, I'm ready to obey, my faithful horse knows what I want to say."

Billy lay limp and completely still until the crowd could bear it no longer. They started calling out to have him brought back to life. Astley bowed and edged his boot nearer the horse's side.

"Rise young Bill . . ."

Billy raised his head, looked about him, and then heaved himself up onto his feet. The crowd, greatly relieved, broke into loud applause.

After this Little Billy had his audience with him all the way. They roared with laughter as they watched him undo his girths, pull off his saddle, and carefully drop it at Astley's feet.

There were delighted giggles as Billy followed his master round the arena sorting out the ladies and the gentlemen by nodding or shaking his head. He picked up a handkerchief, trotted across the arena, and carefully dropped it at the feet of the prettiest girl.

An astonished audience watched him tell the time by striking six o'clock on the ground with his hoof, while Astley's loud running commentary drowned the small click of thumb and finger-nail that was the signal for each stroke.

He went lame, and hobbled about on three legs. Then, miraculously cured, he trotted out of the ring, applause and laughter echoing round him.

Billy had won his way into the hearts of his first audience and started on the road that would lead to the making of his master's fortunes and to his own fame.

It was the start of a tough, hard life. As soon as the summer season was over, Astley packed up and set out with his three horses for the big autumn fairs.

For Little Billy it meant days spent picking his way over the stony, rutted highways of England, carrying a baggage load on his back; and nights spent in strange stables, usually draughty and dirty.

It meant giving his performance in any rough corner of ground, among the clatter and din of the fairs.

It meant facing the autumn gales and driving rain, working on treacherous slippery ground, and getting covered in mud when he lay down.

By the time they reached London again it was late in February. Billy and his companions were put into good warm stables and rested, while their tireless master set to work to find a new show-ground for the summer season.

He found it at the foot of Westminster Bridge—a neglected, overgrown timber yard. Astley rapidly turned it into a permanent show-ground, clearing away the jungle of weeds, roping off a riding arena, setting up benches, and building stables for the horses.

The season opened at Easter—with a bang! This was Mrs. Astley beating the drum. She was followed by Astley on his white charger with trumpet and handbills. The noise they made attracted a lot of attention and the season opened to a full house.

As before, Billy won the hearts of his audience.

The news of the "wonder horse" soon spread and,

before long, crowds were flocking over Westminster Bridge to see him.

Across the river at Pentonville, Zucker's Little Learned Horse might gnash his teeth with rage, for whatever new tricks he did, the Little Military Learned Horse went one better.

When Zucker's Little Horse carried a loaded tea-tray, Little Billy caused a greater sensation by picking a kettle of boiling water off the fire in his mouth to make the tea, which he then served on a tray. He also learned to fire a pistol with his hoof.

The show prospered. Astley bought and trained more horses, and added other performers—clowns, acrobats and tumblers.

Little Billy lived calmly in a world of bustle, noise and excitement. Unmoved by the explosive roar of pistols, unafraid of fire and boiling kettles, he now learned to carry his master through a high school act that ended with a spectacular *piaffe*, in the centre of a ring of fireworks.

Astley himself was afraid of only one thing—the weather. A wet day would empty the seats, and a really bad summer could mean ruin.

He began to dream of the day when he could put a roof over his whole show-ground, turning it into a vast amphitheatre—Astley's Amphitheatre!

That day was to come, but not just yet.

Astley had still to build his reputation before he could build a theatre. Once again, two pieces of luck came to help him.

The first was a dramatic moment outside his

show-ground. A royal procession of horsemen was riding over Westminster Bridge, escorting His Majesty King George III.

The king's horse, fresh and fidgety, took fright and reared up only a few yards from where Astley was standing. Quick as a flash he leaped forward, seized the bridle rein, and saved the royal rider from being unceremoniously dumped in the road.

The king was grateful. The result was an invitation to Astley to give a royal command performance at Richmond.

Under the trees in the park on a warm June evening, Little Billy did his tricks to a cool and critical audience, and warmed them into a response. The show was a success. It led to Astley's second piece of luck—an invitation from the French ambassador to "Monsieur Astley" to entertain the king and queen of France.

In the spring of the following year, Little Billy crossed the Channel with a team of Astley's best horses. For twelve long hours he was shut in the dark heaving hold of the ship as it pitched and rolled across the sea. Terrified and shaking, they landed at Calais, and Little Billy found himself trotting along the straight miles of dusty white roads that led across Northern France to Paris.

The performance was given in the spacious grounds of the royal palace of Fontainbleau. Here, before the ageing king, Louis XV, and a crowd of courtiers that included the most expert horsemen in the country, Astley gave a brilliant display of horsemanship. But, again, it was the Little Military Learned Horse with the endearing tricks who warmed the hearts of the audience and stirred them to a show of enthusiasm. He became a special favourite of the ladies of the court, who found him enchanting.

Astley was now reaching the height of his career. The day came when he was, at last, able to achieve his long-ago ambition.

"No more performances in the rain, Bill!" he said, as he came into the stall at the end of the final show of the season to give the little horse his usual titbit.

The next day, the doors opened to an army of workmen who were to transform the old timber yard.

Astley watched with pride as a great roof was stretched right across the arena, covering seats and stables. He had at last beaten his old enemy, the weather.

On 2nd November, 1780, "*Astley's Amphitheatre*" opened its doors for the first time, and the public flooded in to gasp and gape, and fill the tiers of seats, which were brilliant with scarlet and gold paint.

The roped-off arena had shrunk to a circle, forty-two feet in diameter—the size it still is today. It was bounded by a low wooden wall to hold the barrowloads of fresh sawdust that had been brought up from the old saw-pits. So the first sawdust ring was made.

That night, Little Billy made his entrance to the music of a full orchestra, and went through his act under the light of a huge chandelier slung from the roof. Its glittering glass reflected the flames of a hundred candles. They shone on the glossy coat and well-muscled body of the little brown horse who had now been entertaining audiences for nearly fourteen years.

The first signs of age were beginning to show in the flecks of grey on his muzzle, and the deepening hollows over his eyes. But Little Billy had lost none of the cheeky liveliness that made him such a favourite with the crowds. The walls of the new amphitheatre echoed to their laughter and applause as they watched him wash his feet in a pail of water, and trot round the ring with a napkin in his mouth, playing the waiter.

That night, certainly, old age was still far away. A new chapter was opening in the fortunes of Philip Astley. He had beaten his rivals, and he had the best performing horse in the country.

Billy became the star attraction of the big street parade that now regularly advertised the show. Behind the trumpets, the drums and the riders came a big open carriage, drawn by a pair of horses. Carried in state on the back seat, the Little Military Learned Horse sat up on his haunches like a dog, holding handbills in his mouth that he distributed to the public.

These were the years of success. For Little Billy they meant a regular pattern of an autumn season in London, a winter season in Paris, and spring and summer spent touring the big towns of England.

Then the tide of fortune turned.

In France, the Revolution swept away the glittering world of court and king. Three years later, England was at war with France.

Astley, now a middle-aged man who had been talking of retiring, suddenly came to life and rushed away to rejoin his old regiment, the 15th Dragoons. He was taken on to be in charge of the horses.

Handing over the management of the Amphitheatre to his son John, Astley plunged into a frenzy of preparation for military service across the Channel.

He was in the midst of this when one of his men came to tell him that someone was asking urgently to see him.

"It's a Mr. Saunders, sir. Abraham Saunders."

"Oh!" Astley remembered a fellow showman from long ago, when they were both struggling. He went to greet a shabby-looking man waiting anxiously at the entrance.

"I'm down on my luck . . ." Saunders began and Astley, who was a generous man, put his hand in his pocket.

"No! It's not money," Saunders said quickly. "I came to ask if I could borrow your horse, Little Billy."

Astley's face fell. He would rather have been asked anything but that.

"The public know him so well," Saunders went on. "He'll pull them in. Let me have him—just till I get on my feet again."

"He's getting to be an old horse now," Astley said

unhappily. "He's been with me for more than twenty years."

"I'll take good care of him," Saunders promised. "You know I will. Let me have him—just for a week."

Reluctantly Astley agreed. He went to Billy's stall and untied him.

"There you are." He handed Saunders the rope. "But not more than a week, mind!"

He stood with a heavy heart, watching his old favourite being led away. He felt deeply uneasy.

The week went by. There was no sign of Billy.

"Is he back yet?" This became Astley's first question every time he came into the stables.

The answer was always the same. "No."

Another week passed, and then the news came through. The moment Astley walked into the stables he could sense the unusual silence.

"What's the matter?" he roared. "You've got news of my horse. Come now, out with it!"

The frightened grooms melted into the shadows. It was his son John who finally told him.

"I'm afraid, Father, that Billy has been lost."

He paused, waiting for the furious outburst. Instead he saw his father stagger and reach out to grip a stall post. He neither moved nor spoke as John explained.

It seemed that Saunders was heavily in debt and only three days after he had borrowed Billy his creditors had seized him and thrown him into prison.

"They held a sale of all his horses," John went

on, "and Billy was sold along with the rest. I only heard the news today, and I went round to try to find out who had bought him, but I fear all trace of him has been lost."

Astley stood as though turned to stone. His Billy, the Little Military Horse that he wouldn't have sold for all the money in the land, had been knocked down by some auctioneer's hammer. Where was he now? Who was his new owner? Some ignorant man perhaps, who would only see an aged, nondescript little horse to be overworked, ill-treated, or even sent to the knacker's yard.

Astley turned abruptly and, without saying a word, walked out of the stables.

Billy had gone and with him, it seemed Astley's good fortune, for the following year disaster struck. The Amphitheatre was burned to the ground. Only the horses were saved.

The news reached Astley in Belgium, where his regiment was stationed. He was given leave of absence by his commanding officer, the Duke of York, and hurried home to see the blackened, charred ruin which was all that was left of his life's work.

Astley had to start all over again to rebuilt his theatre. The workmen came in and, all through that winter, week after week, the savings of a lifetime were poured out in wages and materials. Day after day, in all weathers, the massive figure of Astley could be seen on the site, supervising, organising, shouting and driving the men on. By March the miracle was complete. In only six months a brand new theatre had been built—the biggest and most modern building of its kind in London.

On Easter Monday, 16th April 1795, Astley proudly opened his Royal Amphitheatre, under the royal patronage of the Duke of York.

The wheel of fortune was swinging round once more, and the following year it turned full circle.

It was early in September. Two of Astley's riders were strolling through a street in the East End of London on their way back to the Amphitheatre for the evening performance. On this hot, sunny afternoon even this dingy street looked pleasant enough with the sunlight slanting down between the huddled houses, shining on the cobbles where the sparrows pecked, and warming the back of an old brown horse dozing in the shafts of a rickety cart. One of the men gave the horse a casual glance, and then suddenly stopped and stood there, staring.

"What's the matter with you, Tom?" The other man pulled at his arm. "Come on, or we'll be late."

"I say, Jack. I'm a Dutchman if that ain't our Billy!"

"Impossible," said Jack. It was three years now since Billy had been given up as lost.

"I tell you it is." Tom shook himself free. There was something about this sad-looking brown horse in its shabby harness that convinced him it was indeed their Billy.

"It's his size and colour," Jack admitted. "But how can we be certain?"

"I'll try him." Tom knew the signals Astley used

for some of Billy's tricks. He began to click the nails of his thumb and forefinger. The sound carried clearly in the quiet street.

The horse suddenly jerked up his head. They saw him prick his ears. Then, as though obeying some half-forgotten instinct, he arched his neck and began to caper.

"It's him! It's our Billy!" Both men rushed forward, and the next moment the horse was rubbing his head against them.

"He remembers us!" Tom had his arm round Billy's neck.

"Think of the old man's face when we tell him," said Jack.

"When he *sees* him, you mean!" Tom plunged his hand into his pocket to discover how much money he had on him. "We must find his owner at once."

It wasn't difficult. They found him in the nearest pub, sitting behind a large pot of ale. He was astonished when he learned that these two young men were interested in buying his old horse. But he was always ready to make a bargain, so a price was agreed, and the money paid.

"He's a monstrous good-tempered creature," the man told them as he took off Billy's harness. "But he has such odd antics that we call him the Mountebank." He slipped a halter over Billy's head. "There you are, gentlemen!" He handed over their bargain, and the two men led Billy triumphantly away.

In the meantime, in his house next to the theatre, Astley was changing into his best boots, ready for the evening's performance, when his housekeeper tapped on the door.

"There's two men downstairs to see you, sir."

"I haven't time to see anyone," Astley growled. "What do they want?"

"It's a very important matter, sir," she insisted. "I think you should go."

Astley didn't see the twinkle in her eyes. Grumbling and grunting, he pulled on his boots and stumped downstairs.

The front door stood wide open. Through it he caught sight of two of his performers standing in the road. He scowled. Someone was playing a joke.

"What does this mean?"

He strode out of the house, ready to blast the smiles off the men's faces. "What are you . . .?" He broke off, staring, for they had led forward a small brown horse.

"We've found him," they said simply.

"Billy!" At the sound of that well-known voice calling his name, the horse pricked up his ears and whickered. The next moment Astley was beside him, and Billy was rubbing his head against his master, and nuzzling at his pockets as though he'd never been away.

Astley's hand shook as he fondled his old favourite, and his eyes blurred with tears as he listened to the men telling him how they'd found the horse. Swiftly he ran his hand over Billy's legs and body to reassure himself that he was fit and well.

"Wherever he's been these past three years, they've

taken good care of him," was Astley's verdict, and pulling out a handkerchief he blew his nose loudly.

He was deeply moved. All his fortunes were bound up with the life of this little horse.

"Never again does this 'ere horse go out of my stables," Astley vowed, and he himself led Billy to the stall that was to be his home for the rest of his life.

Billy was delighted to find himself among his old companions again. Everyone crowded round to welcome him back. Tom and Jack were generously rewarded.

"Shall you put him in the programme again?" Tom asked.

"I'll have to see if he's forgotten his tricks," Astley replied.

Billy hadn't. Twenty years' training had stamped itself indelibly on his memory. He responded at once to all his master's signals.

The very next evening Astley announced that, by special request, The Little Military Learned Horse would appear, and into the ring trotted the small brown horse that two days' before had been hauling a cart through the East End streets of London. The public had not forgotten their old favourite, and the theatre echoed to their laughter and applause. Astley, watching him go through his tricks with all his old, lively assurance, felt a deep surge of happiness. Billy was back, and from now on good fortune would go with them.

He was right. The Royal Amphitheatre flourished,

and Astley's promise to Billy was kept. He never left the theatre again. Astley himself retired and went to live in Paris, handing over to his son, John. It was John's partner, Mr. Davis, a kind and understanding man, who took special care of the little horse in his last years.

Billy went on performing until he was well over thirty years old. It was Mr. Davis who presented him, and rode him in the ring to do his *piaffe* to music in a circle of blazing fireworks.

But, inevitably, the time came when Billy's legs grew stiff and his back too weak to work. As he got older he lost all his teeth, and Mr. Davis fed him on soaked bread.

He passed his days quietly in his stall among the familiar sights and sounds of the show that had been his whole life. Then, quite peacefully, one night it was all over. They found him in the morning, stretched out in his stall. This time it was not the Sham Death of the Little Military Learned Horse, it was the real thing. He was forty-two years old.

Mr. Davis wrote to Astley in Paris to give him the news. The letter ended. *"We could not bear the idea of losing him altogether so we are having his hide made into a thunder drum for stage effects. It will make us feel that our old friend is still with us."*

The echoes of the thunder drum were to roll through the amphitheatre for nearly a hundred years until, in 1870, the old theatre was finally pulled down to make room for the new St. Thomas's Hospital.

Today there is no trace left of Astley's Amphitheatre, but perhaps on a warm summer night, when Westminster Bridge is quiet, and the river slides silently under it, we can still catch the echoes of drumming hooves, and faraway laughter, as a little brown horse with bold bright eyes comes trotting into a sawdust ring.

SHANDY

by Diana Pullein-Thompson

We once owned a pony called Shandy Gaff. We bought him as a sucker at a sale of New Forest ponies at Reading Market. He had just jumped out of his pen and bloodied his nose falling on hard concrete the other side. He was the colour of lemon shandy with a little white star and trickle down his face, and he cost us seventy-five shillings.

Jumping, we soon saw, was Shandy's speciality. We took him for walks with us like a dog and, although he was then only just over eleven hands, he jumped all the stiles with gusto. He also jumped from field to field at home for sheer enjoyment.

One day Shandy overdid his jumping and slipped his stifle. The vet said he must rest, so we tethered him in the paddock on a rope tied to a stake with a swivel. The stake was driven deep into the ground so that there was no chance that the rope could wind round it. All went well at first, then one afternoon we took Shandy into the kitchen and fed him handfuls of coarse oatmeal from the bin in which it was kept for making porridge. Shandy liked the kitchen. It was warm, with an Aga and red flag-stoned floor.

It was autumn with rain in the air, so that night he

was tethered again in the shelter of a tree. We slept soundly, unaware that the sky was stormy and tempestuous, and in the morning we came down to find the kitchen in chaos. Broken eggs lay on the wet floor, the oatmeal bin was tipped over and empty, a box of cutlery lay upside down amongst the eggs. The door was wide open, for our father had come in late from a meeting and not latched it securely. Who could have caused the chaos? There were little hoof marks here and there on the floor and our first thought was Shandy! But, on looking out of the window, we saw that he was standing docilely beside his tethering stake, back to the wind. The rain had stopped. Yet he was the only pony who knew about the oatmeal bin, although there were others who had come for brief moments into the kitchen.

For a while we were mystified, until the time came to take Shandy a drink and an armful of hay. He wasn't thirsty, the night's rain had wetted him enough, but as he stretched his neck to pull at the hay, we saw that his rope was severed. In a flash we knew what had happened. He had broken free, jumped the palings into the garden, crossed the rosebed and made his way to the kitchen then, after satisfying his curiosity, filling his belly with oatmeal and having a warm-up by the Aga, he had returned to his allotted place.

But why the deceit? Had he a sense of right and wrong? Or did he simply return to be in the right place for his food and drink? We shall never know.

THE PONY WHO THOUGHT SHE WAS A DOG

by Diana Pullein-Thompson

Can you bring up a pony like a dog? Can you domesticate him, house-train him, take him into shops or for a day by the sea, knowing he won't disgrace himself? The question had plagued Cynthia for months, and all at once she decided to solve it. She would try herself, but for convenience' sake the pony must be small.

The decision made, Cynthia went to the Shetland Pony Stud Farm at Daventry, where she chose a black foal, just weaned, whom she named Jan. She travelled home with her new possession snuggling in her arms.

When they arrived at Knowle, in Warwickshire, she put the little black filly out in an orchard by the house, a pleasant place with plenty of grass, for she knew that she would not be allowed to take the foal up to her bedroom like a dog.

Next morning, Cynthia's first thought was of Jan. She sprang from her bed, pulled on clothes, and dashed out into the orchard, bright with the early sun. But the place was empty. Little Jan, homesick for her mother, had gone down on her knees and crawled through a small hole in the hedge. A frantic search followed. So small and dark a person could easily be run over and she had evidently got out on to the road. But she wasn't far away and the hunt finished when she travelled back to Cynthia sitting on a groom's lap, in a furniture van driven by a kindly man who was willing to break his journey for the sake of a lost pony.

Like all young animals, Jan was inquisitive, and very soon found her way into the house. She visited the kitchen first and quickly drank the cat's milk from a saucer on the floor. Later she learned to walk up and down stairs with easy grace, copying the three dogs of the household. She went for walks on a lead, visited the bank and local shops regularly with her mistress, and without any instruction became house-trained. She seemed to know instinctively that it simply wasn't right to leave droppings in the human's stable—perhaps, once again, she copied the dogs.

Cynthia's experiment progressed well, for very soon Jan was taking regular holidays with the family, happily paddling in streams and the sea. Usually she journeyed by car, the front seat being taken out so that she could stand looking out of the back window. Once when Cynthia was on holiday in Wales she missed the absent Jan so much that she wrote home asking for her to be sent as soon as possible. The pony arrived next day by rail, crated like an animal despatched to a zoo, but calm for her trust in humans was becoming absolute. In Wales Jan learned to climb the rough steps made to help walkers over the dry stone walls. She took long treks with the family, keeping up like a dog without a lead, enjoying her share at the picnics.

Like most people of breeding, Jan preferred to travel in style. When asked to collect for charity at a fête she arrived in a Rolls-Royce. On another occasion she was happy with a Daimler. Such large cars were pleasantly smooth and no seat had to be removed so that she could be accommodated. Once she returned from a holiday with Cynthia by train and on arrival at Birmingham's old Snow Hill Station found that there was no car to meet her. Walking home was out of the question because Cynthia had sprained her leg. Jan looked around her, then eyed the waiting taxis hopefully. They looked roomy enough. Why not get in? She waited for Cynthia to step forward and cause a door to be opened. The taxi drivers hesitated. They wanted the fare, for business was slack, but they were not accustomed to taking ponies. Would she kick their cabs or put droppings on the seat? Jan was thirty two inches high, "No bigger than a dog," Cynthia assured them, "*and* just as well behaved." Eventually one taxi-man agreed to take the girl and pony, but first he spread newspaper on the floor, just in case . . . It wasn't necessary. Jan's manners on such occasions were impeccable. She sailed home looking out of the back window as usual.

Home had become the Edgbaston Church of England School for Girls in Birmingham, where Cynthia's aunt was headmistress. Here Jan roamed the corridors like her canine friends, when permitted inside, passing school children on the stairs with great aplomb. The gardens were a delight to her, and the pupils spoiled her when they got the chance. She became in her way a personage of some importance.

But Jan, for all her dog-like habits, liked her own kind, too. She could talk pony language and nibble manes and withers with the best of them, but she remained most at home with humans, and she played with dogs.

After a few years when Jan was mature Cynthia began to dream of another foal, Jan's son or daughter. The local vet, one of the most famous in the Midlands, Brennan Devine, was consulted. Why yes, he agreed, Jan was perfectly fit to become a mother. Come to think of it he had to go over to Daventry himself in a few days and he would be happy to take the pony along with him to meet her future mate. She could travel comfortably in his Rolls-Royce. So Jan returned in style to her birthplace, her feelings unconsulted. There at the stud farm she was treated purely as a pony. There were no trips to the seaside, shopping expeditions or school events to break the monotony. Fenced in with other Shetlands who had never seen the world, she became increasingly bored. Worst of all, she did not like any of the stallions. She was too highly civilised to mate instinctively. For a little pony, so cherished and cushioned against nature's calls, the idea did not make sense.

So Jan went back to Edgbaston unmated, glad to be with her human and canine friends again, petted and pampered, not one of several but a unique being.

A few years later she was destined to take on another job, or perhaps you could say she enjoyed another form of motherhood. Cynthia married and, before long, there was a human baby crawling on Jan's back and reaching up to touch her soft muzzle. The black pony treated her mistress's child with the utmost care, allowing her to crawl by her feet, play with her hoofs and stroke her legs. Cairi grew to love Jan as other little children love puppies. By the time she was four she could ride the little Shetland anywhere, taking her back to the field alone and unsaddling and bridling her for, of course, Jan helped her in every way she could. Cairi and later her younger sister, Corran, grew to love ponies through the kindness of their first, who had nannied them so well.

In later years they both became famous riders in the Midlands. One of them now schools horses, specialising in difficult cases. As for Jan, she lived to be nineteen and is remembered affectionately to this day.

This story was told to Diana Pullein-Thompson by Cynthia Muir

HORSES OF LONG AGO

by Dorothea Cannan

In Queen Victoria's day we lived in Oxford.

I must have been about five or six years old when my mother bought our first pony. She was a small brown mare of no particular breed called Brownie, and my sisters and I loved her very much. She drew the governess cart into which we three little girls were packed with our nurse, and my mother drove us about the then country roads within five miles of where we lived.

Brownie was stabled at an inn called The Lamb and Flag, kept by a Mr. Rhodes, and a groom brought her to the house and was there to fetch her when we came back from our drives.

Later on I was taught to ride by Mr. Rhodes, who walked Brownie and I up and down a country road called Gipsy Lane, a short way out of the town. There he showed me how to hold the reins and how to sit properly on a side saddle. He ran beside Brownie when I was ready to trot, and then took me on a leading rein, riding a horse himself. In those days I wore a *habit*, a sort of skirt made of heavy grey cloth with a jacket to match and a white stock which was worn like a cravat, and, to top it all, a black bowler hat, which would have been quite useless if I had fallen on my head. The habit was cut short at the back, so that it did not hang down on the other side of the pony. When I was on foot, I could pull it round and fasten it with an elastic loop and button, thus making a complete skirt.

When my sisters and I grew too big to ride Brownie she was sold, to our great grief, and Mr. Rhodes took us out on his own horses. My favourite was a bouncy grey mare, called Sweetbriar. Our parents treated us each to a day's hunting every season, sometimes with the South Oxfordshire Hounds and also with the Bicester Hunt. We were not given jumping lessons, but once we were firm at the gallop there was little difficulty in staying on over fences. There was one wonderful occasion when Sweetbriar and I led the field and came in first at the kill. I cannot now imagine how we did it.

There were many horses and ponies in Oxford at that time. A favourite of ours was a big, quiet, brown gelding, which drew the smart brougham belonging to Sir William and Lady Marley. When Lady Marley happened to be calling at our house we used to rush into the street to feed him with sugar. The doctors went their rounds in broughams with a coachman to drive and walk the horse up and down while the doctor saw his patient. The top Oxford surgeon had a splendid dog cart and a very lively horse. If anyone was very ill, straw would be put down in the street or road to deaden the noise of hooves and wheels.

The tradespeople all had carts for their deliveries.

The bakers usually had covered vans drawn by quiet horses, while the butchers used open vehicles and showy horses for they always seemed in a hurry to bring the meat to the houses. The dustmen's horses were very large and slow, for they needed to be patient because they were for ever being stopped while dust-bins were emptied.

On two Oxford streets there were trams, which ran on lines like a railway, each drawn by two horses. Occasionally they came off the lines and the horses had a hard job to get them back on again. A faster form of transport was the bus, also drawn by two horses, which ran between Oxford and a neighbouring village. On market day many people came in to town in the carriers' carts, which had hoods to pull up if it rained.

The quickest way to travel short distances was by cab. These were summoned by the maids by whistle. One blow meant a hansom was wanted, two blows meant a four-wheeler, which was known as a *growler* or a *fly*. If you took a cab from the station, small boys would try to clamber up behind for a ride, or run with it in the hope of getting a few pennies helping with the luggage when you reached home.

There were two Oxford dogs who liked to use cabs. Our own, Jim, a rough-haired brown and white fox terrier, would walk each morning with my father to the office, where he would sleep for a time in front of the office fire. Eventually, feeling bored, he would take his leave, hurry down a quiet street, cross a wide and busy road and jump in a cab at the rank.

Glad to get a fare, the driver would then take him briskly home, where he would be paid for his trouble. Then there was a bulldog known as "Oriel Bob", who belonged to Oriel College. He loved to attend football matches, from which he would return by cab. On delivering the dog to College, the cab driver would be paid by the porter. They must have felt very important, those two dogs in cabs trotting down St. Giles or Cornmarket watching the poorer people trudging home on foot.

Although we were town children, we had experience of country horses too.

We often stayed with our cousins in Scotland. In one place in the Western Highlands there were strong ponies to do the farmwork. There was no road to the estate and when the weather was too rough to reach it by sea loch, the ponies would be taken by mountain paths to the railway station. Here, trunks, suitcases and a large tin box with a lid would be slung either side of each pony, and we and the people who had come to fetch us would walk the six or seven miles to the house. We used to ride these ponies to church where they would wait patiently for our return at the end of the services. They were very sure-footed and took us safely up and down very steep tracks and winding mountain paths.

Most of the horses and ponies you see today are used for pleasure, but when I was a child they were an essential part of life. A lame horse could mean a man out of work or, in the wilder parts of the country, no postal service that day and much more besides.

They were as much part of life as the car is today, and proved to be one of man's hardest-worked servants and best of friends. In the towns we wakened to the sound of their hooves and the jingle of their harness and we loved them for their beauty, and sometimes also for their gentleness and patience.

THE MARE WITH THE BAD WHITE FACE

by Barbara Woodhouse

For a lover of horses the Argentine is the saddest place to live, for these most intelligent and willing animals and servants of men are never treated as they should be, but are roughly handled from the first. I think I learnt to speak fluent Spanish more quickly than usual because of my rages—as when, for example, I saw a brute of a man knock a horse's eye out with one lash, and then laugh. I learnt to unbraid them in no mild language; but all they said was that horses were worth only a few pesos, and they must be taught quickly. Hence the cruel method of breaking a horse in, by lashing it to make it gallop and then pulling it fiercely back on to its haunches, three men and horses all putting a concerted pull on its mouth at the same time. I pleaded with them to be kind, but it had no effect, so I decided to show them that I could break horses as quickly and as well as they could and without any cruelty. I begged the manager of the *estancia* to let me have a three year old to start on, but he refused point blank. "Women don't break horses out here, that is a man's job," he said, and all my pleading fell on deaf ears.

But I don't believe in being defeated in anything I

really wish to do, so I bided my time. Shortly after this the whole of the unit went many miles away out into the camp on a branding job and were away for three days. The only people left were myself, my old Indian cook, and the old native who chopped our logs for us and did all the odd jobs such as butchering. I saw the men off, and then went out to the barn to find old Fernandez. I think he liked me, for I was the only person there who treated him like an ordinary human being and not as a slave. I asked him how long the *capitas* and *patrón* would be away, and he said, "Three sun downs", so I told him that before they came back I wanted to break in a horse to do everything that their own horses could do. He looked at me as if I were mad, but listened to me when I suggested that we should ride out in the camp together to the wild herd and that he should lasso one of the horses for me. I promised him tobacco and pesos, and with much wagging of his head he agreed.

I could hardly wait whilst he ponderously saddled his fat old mare and went to fetch a little bay pony for me. Together we rode out and at last came to the herd. At first they paid no attention to us and we quietly rode round them. Then I saw what I wanted, a beautiful golden chestnut with four white socks and a blaze down her face. I pointed her out to Fernandez but he shook his head. "Don't have her," he said, "she has a *mala cara*," which means a bad white face, and in the eyes of the natives suggests a bad bargain even before you start. But I knew this to be nonsense, and told him to catch her. Neatly the rope encircled her neck, and then she flung herself about like a salmon on a line. But eventually she was tied to the ring in the saddle of his own horse, and his old mount played the youngster like an experienced fisherman. Bit by bit she stopped pulling, and in the end we got her tied up near the house on a rawhide halter and a rope. By this time the old man was terrified of what he'd done and begged me to let her go again, for he said the master would kill him when he came home. I told him it was nonsense; that Englishmen didn't behave like that, and that I myself would take full responsibility. And in any case I had heard the *patrón* telling him before he left to do all that I wanted. Miserably he slunk off to his barn to continue his routine task of scraping the fat and flesh off the sheep skins to make them ready for the tannery. I could hardly believe my luck. Here was this gorgeous creature for me to tame, and no one to say nay to me.

I approached her gently, speaking in a low caressing tone of voice. She flinched at first on my approach and snorted furiously, but did nothing more. I then stroked her nose and her neck, and ran my fingers gently down her mane, for I knew that horses loved this, and soon she stood quite dreamily still; so I then ran my hands down her legs and picked up her feet, talking gently and soothingly all the time. Next I went down her body and picked up her back legs; then round the other side and back to her head. Then I got a sack and gently slapped her all over with it. She leapt in the air with the first feel of it, but soon, when she found it did not hurt her, she paid no more attention to it. I whisked it over her back and under her tummy. I slapped her legs gently, and down her tail. I then dropped the sack off her back until she no longer flinched, and that ended the first lesson. Next I taught her to eat sugar by putting it between her back teeth. At first she spat it out, so the next time I held it in her mouth until it had nearly melted. That worked wonderfully, and in no time she was crunching up as much as I could give her. But I kept it as a reward for everything new that I wished to teach her. I next fetched my saddle and put it on her back with a very loose girth. Up went her back in a terrific buck, but I talked to her and moved the saddle about, and then tightened the girth one hole and made her move. This time she hunched her back but did not buck, so I tightened it up to make it safe, and then got an old wood block and put it by her side, so that I could stand on it and lean heavily over her, talking all the while. She never stirred, so gently I swung my leg over her and slid on and off about three times like this. I then put reins on the side pieces of her head-collar, since I do not believe in bits, and I sat on her back whilst she was still tied up. Next I urged her forwards a pace or two, and then said "Ssh" and pulled her to a stop on the reins. Encouraged by her docility I slipped off the rope she was tied up with, and leant over to pull her gently on the head-collar to urge her forward. She walked on, and after half an hour of this I unsaddled her and took her out into the small paddock by the house and tied the long rope to a movable tree trunk and let her wander. At first she was terrified of the log moving along after her, but soon she got accustomed to it. After lunch I brought her in again and rode her for another half an hour. Soon she was trotting and walking well, but I still had the feeling that she might panic at any minute.

Anyway, to cut a long story short, by the end of the three days this pony was going extremely well. I opened the gates of the corral, told old Fernandez to follow me at a distance, and off I went on her for my first ride. It was without incident for some time, until something frightened her in the grass, when she put herself into a series of bucks that would have done credit to a buck-jumping contest. I was ready for it, for all the time she had felt to me as if the slightest error on my part would make her try to get rid of me. However, we came home safely, and I caressed her lovingly and let her free in the small paddock near the house. Next morning I rode alone for an hour, and so her breaking continued smoothly.

On the last day before the men came home, I met an old Guarani Indian*, riding a beautiful little bay mare. We stopped and said polite things to each other, and I told him I was taming the chestnut I was on. He said he thought only his own tribe knew the secret of taming horses without fear, and, when asked what it was, he told me to watch the next time I turned strange horses out together and see what they did. I asked what he meant, and he told me that horses always

* Guarani: peaceable tribe of South American Indians, having their home chiefly in Paraguay and Uruguay and on the Brazilian coast.

go up to each other and sniff each other's noses, which is their way of saying "How do you do?" in their language, and that hc always did the same thing when he wished to tame a horse himself. He said: "Stand with your hands behind your back and blow gently down your nostrils. Keep quite still, and the horse will come up to you and sniff and will blow up your own nose, after which all fear will have left him. That horse, providing that you don't give it reason to turn vicious, will always be your friend and the friend of man." And with that he cantered off at the easy gallop of the perfectly matched horse and rider, with his reins hanging loosely and without a saddle, just a blanket on the horse's back.

That evening the men came home and I told them what I had been up to, and of course got the most severe scolding possible. Fernandez was threatened with the sack, but I pointed out that it was my fault entirely and that he had been ordered to do what I wanted. No more was said until I gave a little show with my *mala cara*, who behaved like a lamb, and the manager said he supposed I could break a horse. I felt this was the moment to ask for another, for I was dying to try out the Guarani's trick. So another was caught up for me. I sniffed up her nose and immediately stroked her and saddled her up. From her behaviour she might have been an old horse, for she never flinched or snorted or showed any sign of fear. I cut out the preliminary sack flapping and fondling and gently mounted her, loosed the rope, and with my heels urged her on. She went smoothly with me, and I never for a second had that feeling that I had had with the other horse, that at any minute she and I might part company. In twenty minutes in the corral I taught her to stop, and to turn, and to trot, and then I asked the men watching me to open the gate and away we went. In an hour she was cantering, turning, stopping, and allowing me to mount and dismount without any protest or signs of fear.

I knew the Indian was right, for that horse never put a foot wrong and in three days was a completely trained pony. I could safely round up cattle with her, open and shut gates, and so on; and all this on a head-collar only. I never bitted my horses until much later on, when I knew that they knew what to do from my voice alone. I have won many a bet in England that I would do anything normal on a horse without saddle or bridle, winning simply because I knew that my horse knew every command of voice. For a bet, I have played fast polo on reins of one strand of "50" cotton. My success with the Guarani's trick gave me the chance in life I had always wanted, for from now on, instead of the *peons* being paid to tame the horses, they were given more useful jobs, like fencing, to do, and I was promoted to be horse-breaker at ten shillings per horse. The Inspector of the cattle company was told about me and came out later to see why a woman was allowed to do this. He rode one of my horses that had been completely untouched two hours before and could find no fault in it except lack of experience. It was thus that I became the happiest woman on earth in my self-chosen job.

LOST IN THE MOORS

by Diana Pullein-Thompson

The road that runs from Elvanfoot to Moffatt in the lowlands of Scotland, not far from the English border, was no place for a rider, even in the 'fifties, when, with a girl called Ailsa Ravencroft, I rode from John O'Groats to Land's End, so that we should know our own country from top to bottom. It wasn't very long since I had lain in bed for almost a year with tuberculosis, when it was a much-feared disease, for which rest was part of the cure, and I think I also wanted to prove to myself and my relations that I was now completely fit and well.

On that particular day when I was lost on the moors, Ailsa's horse, aptly named None The Wiser (for although pleasant-looking he never seemed to learn any sense), had lost his nerve, hating the foul-smelling lorries which pounded their way through the Scottish landscape, and I had gone on alone after arrangements had sadly been made for him to follow by horsebox. I didn't *feel* alone because I had the company of Favorita, and if I spoke to her she always put back one elegant flea-bitten grey ear to catch my words.

It wasn't agreeable for either of us as we made our

way along the shining tarmac, regretting the absence of a verge and flinching at the noise and the smell of the traffic. The drivers cared nothing for a solitary rider—many came so close that damp dust spattered us, and the motorbikes irritated us almost beyond endurance. And all the time to our left lay the great tempting moors of Moffatt, desolate, empty and quiet but for the call of the curlews and the distant baaing of sheep.

My map showed a Roman road, a track that ran almost all the way, it seemed, to Moffatt, which was a mile from the place where I had arranged to meet Ailsa at half-past six. No one had been able to tell me whether the way was still open, for no one but the shepherds walked the moors and none of them were to be found. But at Elvanfoot there had been people who were optimistic.

"Och, as likely as not it'll be open," they told me. "It's a grand ride when the weather's all right." But I knew from experience that there were Scotsmen who, when in doubt, said what they thought you wanted to hear.

It wasn't long, however, before the contrast between the busy, exasperating road and the brown sweep of moorland was too much.

"Nothing venture, nothing win," I told myself, turning up a track that led through a farmstead right to the Roman road.

As I went, my heart lifted and a new spring came into Favorita's long, swinging stride. It was lovely to escape the traffic at last, to canter across damp green fields, with the cool heather-scented breeze in my face and the wide clear sky above, streaked with soaring birds, touched by pale sunshine.

Soon I left the pasture and came to the bleaker moors that seemed to stretch for miles and miles, undulating like corrugated cardboard. Large trees gave way to stunted rowans and then to myrtle; the land grew browner, softer, the grass sparse. For a time the track was there, leading me onwards like a kind friend, and Favorita, my good grey mare, hurried on eagerly with pricked ears and bright eyes.

She had seen so much: a wild and angry sea at John O'Groats; the cold April sleet falling on the long straight road from Wick; Dunrobin Castle white as icing sugar, shuttered and turreted, a landmark for sailors. She had slept anxiously in its stables which she had believed haunted and in countless alien fields, stables and stalls. She had come through Drumochter Pass and stared wonderingly at the lofty Grampians and the naked hideousness of the hydro-electric developments. She had waited impatiently outside shops while we bought provisions, drunk deeply from burns and rushing rivers and buckets brought by well-wishers on the way. Now her Arab blood from the Royal Stud of Hungary which gave her courage, intelligence and a strong, impatient will, was to be tested in the wild, bog-ridden country that lay before us. But, although she could not be expected to have the native sense of an Exmoor or Fell pony, she had learned stoicism as a second whipper-in's horse, turning back into woods to bring out lost or lagging hounds while all her friends galloped on. As a brood mare she had gained a certain calmness and, in dressage tests, some self control.

Presently the Roman road narrowed, becoming, I thought, too winding and uncertain to be genuine, and, when we had covered about seven miles, it petered out. Now the shadows were lengthening with late afternoon. Round and beautiful, the sun was drifting behind clouds in the western sky. There were great gullies—the dips in the corrugated cardboard—which were to plague us all the way, and then, quite suddenly, quite horribly, a shining, glinting, brand new barbed wire fence stretching like a thin silver scar to right and left across the landscape as far as the eye could see.

I felt a sudden catch at the heart, as you can guess. Should I turn back and retrace the seven miles to that horrible road? No, I hate turning back. It goes against the very core of my nature. But if there was no path, how could I find my way across the moors? Supposing night came down and I rode in mad circles? Well then, I should come back here to the fence and perhaps pick up the track again and then the road, guided by the lights of the long-distance lorries making their way to England. A compass? I realised then, with a twinge of anger at myself, that I had left it with Ailsa. Determined to travel light, I had emptied a heap of belongings from my saddle bags for her to take in the horsebox. But I had a map, two miles to an inch; the sun was still visible in the changing sky, and my watch still ticked.

right
Pit Ponies

below
Jan, the Shetland who thought she was a dog

left, above
Haydon's portrait of Wellington's war horse, Copenhagen *(photo: Courtauld Institute)*

left, below
Monica Dickens and John

right
Diana riding Favorita

below
A Victorian ride – Dorothea Cannan in Oxford

left
A magnificent jump – Christine Pullein-Thompson on Lorraine

below
Red Rum ridden by Ron Barry

"When in doubt, go *on*," I told myself. "Never turn back."

The posts rose eight inches above the wire, so I knew what to do, to lessen the chance of an accident. I fished Favorita's halter out of a saddle bag and tied it from one post to another where the ground seemed firmest. Then I unrolled my macktintosh and hung it over the halter, making that part of the fence into a formidable-looking jump. The top was now some six inches higher than the highest strand of wire and if Favorita made a mistake, which wasn't likely, she would probably hit the rope, which might cause her to fall but would not cut her. The obstacle had a solidness which would make her stand back and take care. She had never yet hit any jump hard enough to bring her to her knees. And she was no fool. She had jumped the timber waggon you can see in the photograph of Lorraine often without hesitation or fault. If anything, she was over-careful.

I mounted her again and, without waiting for any command, she swung round and took me over the jump (for had she not in her youth waited many a time while I made her obstacles out of petrol cans and rustic poles?). She landed heavily and the soil under her hoofs gave way with awful sucking noises, but she righted herself and with an effort pulled herself out and waited to be congratulated with a pat and word of praise.

Halter and mackintosh back in their places, we continued on our way, stopping every now and then to consult the map, sun and watch. It was now ten minutes past five, so I presumed the sun would soon be due west and chose my direction accordingly, but the contours worried me, and I wished I had listened more carefully during geography lessons at school. Perhaps if I had grasped the nettle of longtitude and latitude more thoroughly I could have found the map more useful now that I was lost.

There only seemed to be crazy sheep paths that wound here and there and took us nowhere. The sheep who made them having been concerned with picking the best fodder and not with finding their way to Moffat, or anywhere else for that matter, except perhaps to water when the hot August sun beat down on the shadeless acres. We were forced to make our way across untrodden land, where the ground grew softer the further we went until it squelched under us like a sponge being squeezed of water.

Frightened of bogs, and already seeing Favorita sinking from sight before my very eyes, I dismounted and walked ahead, testing the ground as we went. But she was impatient to finish the journey and enjoy a feed of oats. She felt the first whispers of night in the soft air and heard it in the last eerie calls of the curlews. It was all I could do to keep her behind me and she made the most ridiculous suggestions about which direction we should take, not aware that we were heading for Moffatt—or so I hoped. It is amazing how small and solitary you feel when lost in open landscape, how wide the sky seems and how quickly dusk comes.

I wanted to keep the great curve of the highest hill

to my left. I wanted to see another road, marked on the map as leading down into Moffatt, but there was nothing except the corrugated cardboard, and the sky, now empty of birds, and the golden glow of sunlight. Hues of grey and brown don't lighten the spirits and lift the heart. My thoughts became gloomy and Favorita only wanted to be off the moor and heading for—where? Home, I supposed, still hundreds of miles away.

The gullies grew deeper, sharper and more frequent, their steep sides made hazardous by boulders. Little streams of peaty brown water gurgled fitfully through their bowels. Myrtle grew on their banks.

I hated them, each one seemed worse than the last and the descent was always difficult with Favorita on my heels. Her patience was almost at an end. She wanted to go first, knowing she could manage the boulders without my guiding hand, and, after a while, I let her loose, to find that she always waited for me on the other side, taking the opportunity to pull at the heather and the sparse, nearly colourless grass.

I do not know how many miles we covered in this manner or whether I always kept in the direction I intended. When the ground was firmer I rode, and we made better time. Our side of the world passed the sun's rim, and the sky became blank and greyer still with the approach of night. The moors lay silent before me, hateful, treacherous and cruel, a place where people could die for lack of shade or shelter and sheep lay in winter deep in snowdrifts. With two sweaters under my coat I was warm, and, with spring far advanced, I was not much afraid of a night in the open, but I thought of Ailsa with None The Wiser dragging her around at the end of his halter rope on that little road beyond Moffatt. She would be waiting outside Oakridge Farm, just a name on the map to us and the point we had chosen as our meeting place, perhaps thinking of search parties. And how tiresome to be the cause of a search party, to be so inefficient that people had to forsake their leisure hours to comb the moors for someone who should have known better than to venture there alone without a compass. We had eaten digestive biscuits and cheese for lunch, but now, with my stomach rumbling, hunger added to the gloom.

My map reading was a failure. The road I wanted was not even on the skyline. Even allowing for obstacles and a break of fifteen minutes to rest I should have crossed the moors by six o'clock. It was now half-past, and the moors seemed endless. The very sight and smell of them began to fill me with disgust. And the brown hill on my left was a traitor, not being where the map told me it should be.

My mother was fond of saying, "Always darkest before dawn," and it was this thought which consoled me as I rode down yet another gully, skirting the boulders, hitting angrily at an innocent twig of myrtle with my stick. As I came up the other side, I felt my heart lift again, for there, a few hundred yards away, was another road, black and stretched out across the landscape like a snake reaching to snatch its prey.

Never have I welcomed a road more ardently. Standing in my stirrups, I could see a few cars passing along it like insects on a curve of black earth, and, now and then, a lorry. I patted Favorita's firm, freckled neck.

"You'll soon be gobbling oats, and thank you for being so good," I said.

She wouldn't wait for me to look at the map, or rather I could have *made* her, but I didn't. After all, she had suffered enough already on the long and tedious journey over terrain for which she had not been bred. I would still be late, but probably only an hour or so and I would reach Moffatt well before dark. The ground seemed firmer to my now optimistic eyes, and I pushed Favorita into a trot so that we soon reached the road, which was wide and curving with a white line down the middle. And then my heart went down again, for I saw that my old enemy was there, older than the last one of its kind and rusty here and there, but firm—another barbed wire fence. And I couldn't jump Favorita over this one because there was no verge to the road and that meant we would have to land on the slippery tarmac.

Dismounted, I walked up and down, rocking posts to see if one was loose, but they were all strong and resisted me like rocks. I wished I was a huntsman with clippers attached to a dee on my saddle. I would have to follow the fence until I found a gap or a gate, but would I find one? And which way to go, right or left? And which road was it on the map, this or that? I felt bemused. Had I started to go in circles?

Could it be the road I had left just after half past two, or the one I wanted? And which hill was that? All at once my self-confidence had gone. I waved to the motorists in the hope that one would stop and offer help, but although some waved back gaily, others ignored me and none stopped. Favorita dragged at the reins, then rubbed her head against me, nearly knocking me over. My legs began to feel like lead, and my heart scarcely lighter, when suddenly Favorita's head went up and I heard a welcome sound.

It was like hearing the bark of a lost dog and knowing that he is still alive, such was my relief. Looking into the brown distance, I saw a two-legged figure coming down a hillside, and on his left, pale dots which were the gathering sheep.

"Hi, Help! Hi, Help!"

The wind was against me, pushing back the sound.

"Holt, holt," called the shepherd.

I turned Favorita round to face those specks in the distance. "A grey horse is a wonderful landmark," I said, as she stood like a statue, watching, her head very high, clean-cut in profile, with a wide cheek and a forehead so broad that a brow band had had to be made specially for her. Her face tapered sharply to a delicate muzzle the colour of the underside of field mushrooms, pinky grey, soft and plushy. Now her nostrils were wide and her breath came quickly as she sniffed the air and listened to the shepherd whistling to his dog.

I remounted, waved with both arms and gave a loud holloa, for suddenly the shadow of dusk had fallen over the hills, heralding the darkness which was soon to come. Should I ride down and meet the shepherd, or wait for him and rest my horse? Favorita, excited by the new hope she felt in me, the whistling and the moving sheep, decided the matter by breaking into a brisk trot. And that was our undoing for, before I had even picked up the reins, I felt her sinking and heard the ominous squelch of ground sucking us downwards.

In such moments I die a thousand deaths, and now in my imagination the treacherous peaty substance was in my mouth, the liquid blinding my eyes and stifling my breath, and the sounds of life dimmed for ever in my ears.

But instinct always comes to the rescue. Without conscious thought, I flung myself clear, landing on squelchy ground yet out of the bog. But what of Favorita? Her dismayed dark eyes were looking straight into mine and there was no fight in them, only that pained surprise, as though she was saying, "Where have you taken me *now*? What have you done?"

"Up, up, Favorita! Come on, up, up."

In that wide expanse of land and sky my voice was a sad trickle of sound. "Up, up!"

As I had flung myself clear I had at least had the sense to bring the reins with me, and now I pulled on these by way of encouragement, my heart hitting my ribs in hammer blows.

"Come on, up, up!"

But the sludge was rising higher on her flea-bitten

grey sides, over the elbows it went and above her stifles. Was there no bottom? Were bogs without end?

Here, disappearing before my very eyes, was the horse I had bought as an iron-grey four-year-old, a mare sold cheap because she was going to be difficult to break, having an awkward temperament, it was said. And now she was more than a horse to me, because over the years we had shared so many adventures. She was a friend struggling for her life, far from home and those kinder Chilterns where she had spent the greater part of her life.

I loosened the reins, thinking she might wish to use her neck as a pivot, and said a silent prayer, and she sank further so that the sludge rose to the bottom of the saddle flaps.

"Up, up, Favorita! Come on, up!"

I made as though to hit her, and suddenly the light in her eyes changed, the heavy look of dismay vanished and was replaced by one of fear, then terror. She began to kick and to struggle as though she had come out of a dream into terrible reality. She threw her head about. She floundered and heaved and puffed and panted, her nostrils wide, her sides heaving, and somewhere she must have hit firmer ground, for all at once I saw her chest again. She moved forward as well as upwards; her girth was visible, her elbows, dark with the liquid of the bog; her knees chocolate brown. Never have I been gladder to see knees, tendons, and a pair of fine fetlocks.

Then she was free. She was out, scrambling to

firmer ground, her breath coming like air from a blacksmith's bellows, her eyes protruding like great marbles, glassy with fear.

"Oh, Favorita. Oh, Favorita!"

What does one say on such occasions? I patted her a score of times. I put my arms across her neck and cuddled her. And then I noticed the dark blood like blackcurrant juice oozing from a puncture by a tendon. A punctured vein? How many more trials were to be sent to us? Had I a good strong handkerchief, a pencil or a stick to make a tournique? I put my thumb on the wound and pressed, and after a time the bleeding stopped. The puncture was deep, but the vein was uninjured as far as I could see.

Now the whistling of the shepherd was louder. Looking round, I saw he was a couple of hundred yards away and coming at last in our direction. I waved my arms and shouted. He left the dog looking after the sheep and came striding towards us with that spring in his step which belongs only to men who spend many hours on the hills walking across heather, and moss and myrtle. Handsome and aquiline, with a crook in his hand, he stood looking down on me as though I was a freak gone wilfully astray.

I was beginning to feel a little incoherent.

"She's cut her leg. We landed in a bog. Can you help? I want Moffatt. I have a friend to meet in Moffatt."

His dark angular face showed no emotion, as though people like me were common and tiresome occurrences that interrupted an honest and hard-working man's work.

"Is it far—Moffatt, I mean?"

"It's a wee way to be sure, nine miles when you reach the road."

"Nine miles!"

"Och, maybe a little less."

"And how can I get on to the road? I mean—the fence . . . I want to be quick because of my horse's leg. You see it's swelling already."

"I saw you earlier. I thought you knew the way."

"So did I."

He wasn't a horseman. He couldn't have been, because he didn't even glance at the wound. He waved a long arm.

"Go up that way, and at the top of yon hill there's a gate, which will take you out on the old Edinburgh road."

"Like that, diagonally?" I pointed.

"Yes, and when you get through the gate, follow the fence down to the road, and keep going down all the way to Moffatt."

"How do I avoid bogs?"

"Keep to the sheep paths."

"But they wind this way and that."

"Och." He gave a gesture of impatience, a frown lying like a ridge across his weather-tanned celtic brow. "Keep to the dry land."

"Thank you."

"Avoid the brown patches," he added, allowing the smallest of smiles.

"There was a brand new barbed wire fence across the right of way," I said, encouraged.

"Put up a month back," he replied.

"Well, goodbye then."

We set off up the hill, which was steeper than it looked, and as we climbed the land grew firmer, but Favorita was lame so I would not ride. At the top there was no gate, only the same rusty fence.

I felt near tears. Nine miles to go when we reached the road, and tomorrow sixteen miles to Lockerbie and then Gretna Green, and my horse was lame! The total journey to Land's End was to be between eight and nine hundred miles in all and we were not even halfway and . . . and . . .

But what was the use of letting one's thoughts run in that vein? "Deal with the matter in hand," I told myself. And then I was lucky, for I spotted a broken strand of wire and saw that a slim verge ran along the road on the other side. The highest remaining strand was only about two feet nine inches off the ground, so I draped my mac across it and tried to make Favorita follow me over, but she jibbed. In exasperation I mounted, and then she jumped it at once, lame though she was.

At last we were on the road. Dusk was far advanced and passing cars had their lights on. My feet were blistered but I wasn't tired once I knew I was on my way to Moffatt. The sticking plaster was with Ailsa, but in a saddle bag I had a pair of socks with leather soles which someone had given me, and I quickly exchanged these for my jodphur boots. The air was fresh, the cars were few and, far away down in the valley, I could see lights coming on like the first stars, golden and twinkling. Favorita was limping but cheerful, and occasionally she stopped to snatch some grass. Eight o'clock came and I had a look at the map, to see that I had come from Bog Hill and that on my left was the Devil's Beef Tub, a black abyss surrounded by four hills where the Annandale loons used to hide their stolen cattle. Here, too, in 1745, a Highlander had escaped capture and almost certain death by wrapping himself in his plaid and rolling like a hedgehog to the bottom of the Tub. I did not envy him the journey down.

Eight o'clock, nine o'clock, and there was a police car, climbing the hill towards me. It drew to a halt.

"Miss Ravencroft's companion?"

"Yes, I suppose you could call me that."

"She said if we met you to say she was settled in at Oakridge Farm. Everything is arranged. You take the right turn the other side of the town."

"Thank you. How far?"

"A mile and a half to the farm."

"But to Moffatt?"

"Four or so."

"Four!"

"Well, maybe a wee bit less, three and a half, perhaps."

"I shall need a vet."

"The farmer will help you."

They drove away, and below me lay the valley, where I could now make out whitewashed cottages, dark firs, with the lights increasing as the curtain of darkness came down from the hills. I let Favorita graze for a time, taking the bit out of her mouth, and then we continued on our way.

Those last four miles seemed interminable, and my legs began to ache. But at last we were in the sleepy town and, catching sight of myself in a shop window, I realised how ridiculous and bedraggled I looked. Vanity made me put on the boots again, drag a comb through my hair and set my crash hat straight. I took the right turn and passed through kinder domesticated country with large trees, then I saw an old car approaching, and, beside the moustached driver, a familiar face.

"Found at last!"

Ailsa stepped out, blue-eyed, blonde, with her thick hair plaited into a pigtail. "What happened?"

"My mother has everything ready for you," said the man with the moustache. "The beds are made up and tea is on the table."

The man's name was Cameron Rankin, and he had a bull pen waiting for Favorita to share with None The Wiser, and, in no time, he was bathing her wound, while she was deep in a bucket of the best Scots oats.

So the long day ended by a warm fire with high tea at half-past ten at night, boiled eggs and scones, baps and cakes, and Cameron Rankin's father telling us tales of Nottingham where he had been brought up.

I learned that they had found Ailsa at the gate and offered hospitality, having read about our journey in the newspaper, and would accept no payment. In the morning, the vet came and packed Favorita's wound with penicillin, bandaged it, and injected her against tetanus, and by afternoon we were on our way, for I was told that walking would stop her leg stiffening. I led her the sixteen miles to Lockerbie, and we put up at a large hotel, a once-only extravagance, with a park in which the horses spent the next morning.

The following day Favorita was sound, and we rode on to Gretna Green—where not one of the famous blacksmiths knew how to shoe a horse.

It was summer when we reached Land's End on schedule, forty-two days after we left John O'Groats. While we admired the great white-crested waves of the Atlantic, an uninvited R.S.P.C.A. Inspector looked at the horses and declared them very fit.

There had been many fearful, happy and moving experiences on the journey. But the most frightening still exists for me in those moments, when a dismayed Favorita sank down in the bog and I stood by utterly helpless, holding the reins.

JIMMY AND TIGGY

by Eric Squires

One young pony driver, Jimmy, was a misfit in the mines, a thin and very pale lad who would have been better suited to office work. When his pony, Tiggy, took a hiding from the men he worked for, Jimmy would feel it personally. He would cringe and cry out with each blow the pony received. Quite apart from his extreme sensitivity, Jimmy was a weakling; however, he was very well liked and could tell a very good dirty joke with perfect timing.

Jimmy's main trouble was his reluctance to drive his pony hard within the animal's limits, Tiggy had only to breathe more heavily and Jimmy would rest him. He would often ease the pace, cut the load, and even push full tubs himself rather than work Tiggy harder. The more he did these things, though, the more often he invited trouble from the men. They depended upon the pony for their living and would force the animal into greater efforts. A vicious circle therefore existed, with Jimmy resting the pony and the men overworking it.

Such a situation could not last; the men, quite naturally, complained and asked for another driver. Jimmy was given the chance to change his ways but, even under threat of dismissal, he persisted in molly-coddling Tiggy to a ridiculous extent. We tried unsuccessfully to talk Jimmy into more sensible use of his pony, which had become lazy and awkward to handle. Matters came to a head when Tiggy took a beating from the men. Jimmy complained to the deputy; but, ironically, it was the lad who suffered.

For him to be taken off pony driving was like stopping him from breathing; I well remember his tears when we talked over his troubles one evening. His one ambition had been to drive a pit pony and, perhaps because of his frail body, to prove that he was capable of working down the pit like the rest of us. Now, to have everything taken away from him and be told that his future did not lie in working underground, was a slap in the face for him.

He went to work on a farm, but this proved too strenuous, and eventually ended up in some kind of office. But he did not desert Tiggy completely; and often gave his new driver a quarter-pound of jelly babies to give him. During the evenings, when the lads gathered to drink a sly pint of beer, Jimmy would join us and listen keenly to our stories. The conversation, however, always drifted towards Tiggy, with his driver giving a detailed account of the work day.

What a reunion there was in the pit fields when we drivers took our ponies there for their two weeks holiday! There were very high spirits all round; some of the ponies frisking and galloping around the field like crazy creatures, with a few just nibbling at the fresh green grass, others trotting on the resilient turf and seeming unable to believe in their freedom. But one pony did not enter into the festivities; Tiggy did not leave Jimmy's side.

During the holiday, Jimmy could always be found in or near the fields, and where he was Tiggy would be; that pony had no thought for any other being except his old friend. Jimmy lavished attention on the pony, even taking a horse brush along and grooming him every Sunday.

After that first holiday on the surface, when Tiggy had returned to the pit, Jimmy could not make physical contact with the pony and only by sending small goodies down to him could he keep a weak hold on his dream. Jimmy just could not obtain enough information about Tiggy and, when another driver took over the pony, he, too, was drawn into our friendly circle to talk about "Jimmy's pony".

We were at that age when we were too young to go into a pub and drink, but, like most of the mining village youngsters, we had our adult friends who willingly purchased a bottle or two of "Taddy's Nut Brown Ale" for us to take to the playing fields. Jimmy paid out more than his share by buying extra bottles, toffees and cigarettes; Tiggy had now become an obsession with him.

Early in the following year, Jimmy fell ill with rheumatic fever and, apart from the occasions when we visited him during his recuperation, we saw nothing of him until he was allowed out of doors for brief periods. His illness had weakened him further, he looked ill—he was ill. But he never complained to us when he continued his demands for news of Tiggy. His driver always told Jimmy the good side, that Tiggy was an obedient pony, he was strong, clever and willing and a sheer joy to handle. Jimmy did not know that Tiggy had in fact become difficult; not that he was an angry pony, but that he made trouble by moving when he should have held, by standing still and refusing to pull when ordered.

However, on the day that the ponies were due to be brought out of the pit for their annual holiday, Jimmy was waiting at the bottom of the lane leading to the pit fields. We were not supposed to ride the ponies to the fields but we did—sometimes riding one and leading another. The utter exuberance of those ponies when they breathed the fresh air, felt the warmth of the sun and quivered their nostrils at the scent of the green grass and other long-forgotten smells was wonderful to witness.

When I arrived with my pony and another at the bottom of the lane, I saw Jimmy, his face pale, haggard and hollow-eyed, with tears running in tiny rivulets, as he looked past me at the pony behind, at Tiggy. The driver dismounted, intending to lead the pony to Jimmy, but that proved to be unnecessary. Tiggy led the way and, ignoring the field gate a few yards beyond, went straight to his friend and nuzzled him with an affection that I know I will never witness again. Jimmy cried, the tears streaming down his face as, with his fingers closed around the halter band, he reciprocated with silent strokings that spoke a million words.

A pony brought out of the pit becomes a changed animal, particularly the older ones which have known this moment before. They gallop this way and that in sheer joy, speeding in one direction to halt and prance, then galloping off again. But Tiggy did none of this. He stood quietly and rumbled his greetings between nuzzling and accepting the tit-bits offered, flicking his lips at Jimmy's face and chesting close to him.

Jimmy led Tiggy into the field and removed his halter, then, standing back, he offered the pony his freedom along with the other ponies, but he did not move away, instead, he turned back towards Jimmy and stayed there near the fence. Jimmy encircled Tiggy's head in his arms and pulled him close, his thin shoulders still heaving somewhat because of his crying, but his head held high with fierce pride.

Eventually, Jimmy decided that Tiggy was entitled to his freedom, and went to the gate which he closed behind him, with the pony neighing and shaking his head violently. He wanted Jimmy's presence and love more than the green grass, more than the proffered freedom and the expanse of running space. Halfway along the lane Jimmy joined us as we moved into a field on the left to take the short cut home, and only then did Tiggy lower his mouth to the lush grass for the first time. He chomped on a mouthful as he watched us disappear into the distance.

During the two weeks' holiday, Tiggy was always

waiting at the fence for Jimmy. Regardless of what time we went to feed the ponies, he was always standing there a little to the right of the gate. Tiggy knew when Jimmy was coming, though the pony could not see him until we had topped a rise to come into view, and the lad never gave any indication of his approach by whistling or calling out.

Tiggy knew more than we knew, more than Jimmy or his parents knew, and infinitely more than Jimmy's doctor knew. Just a few short months after Tiggy returned to the pit, Jimmy died suddenly. His previous illness had taken its toll and his heart failed.

Because of his awkward behaviour when working, Tiggy had been given an easy task on the night shift. His driver was an elderly man, who had been a pony driver nearly all his mining life, and was accustomed to talking to his pony as though he were another human.

One night, when Tiggy was standing beside a spare prop on which his driver was seated, he became restless and began to swing his hindquarters from side to side in a most unusual fashion; he pawed the ground constantly with first one then the other hoof. He became so agitated that he sidled over and trod on the old man's foot. The driver searched for reasons as to why Tiggy was restless, but found nothing. The roof was well supported and there was no bitting. There was no haulage rope nearby and, therefore, no moving tubs to upset the pony. The harness was correctly fitted and there appeared to be no physical reasons why Tiggy should behave so curiously.

The pony began to voice some sort of discomfort, with low whinnies and rumbles, and the old man decided that Tiggy was ill. He checked his watch and noted the time to be just a few minutes after midnight then, trying to console his pony with soothing words, he said, "It's only a few minutes after midnight and I can't take you back to the stables without authority. Anyway," he went on, "there's no stableman there and I wouldn't know which pony to exchange you for."

Suddenly, Tiggy ceased his restlessness and stood in complete silence for some minutes; then, shaking his head hard, he neighed four times very loudly, then stood with lowered head in a dejected attitude.

Jimmy died at exactly ten minutes past twelve that same night.

I am convinced that Tiggy knew of Jimmy's passing. He knew that day at the pit fields that Jimmy did not have much longer on this earth, and his knowledge was shown in the manner he fussed over the lad. Perhaps the simplicity of two words will qualify what there was between Tiggy and Jimmy, and these are simply: *good* and *perfect*!

Such a very special relationship as this between boy and pony does not occur often. From my personal experience in working with ponies, however, I know there are definite steps which can be taken to improve your pony's lot and your association with him.

Get to know your animal. Take time out to study your own human friends and note the essential differences between them and yourself. Check on the physical differences, *and* the mental characteristics, that go towards making each pony an individual. Learn by heart his little traits and whims, his likes and dislikes, and do not force upon him that which he clearly cannot stomach—by doing so your relationship can never be truly satisfactory. After all, if you do not like heights or being shut in, no one would dream of forcing you to climb the sheer side of a mountain or lock you in a tiny, dark room.

When a so-called "bad pony" succumbs to love and affection and becomes quiet in your presence, that is a moment of pure satisfaction. There are ponies with quick tempers, and why not? Are there not many people with this failing? The same goes for ponies with a lazy outlook on life, but these faults do not give licence for an animal to be beaten into submission. I am proud of the fact that I never once beat a pit pony, despite being threatened by flying hooves and slashing teeth. I found that an animal nearly always responded to love and affection, even, to some extent, the very difficult ones.

Nothing is so wonderful as seeing your pony running to you because he loves you; lifting off your cap and asking for a tit-bit, or flapping his lips at your face and rumbling a greeting. Nothing can compare with the pleasure of the moment when your pony lays his head upon your shoulder and looks at you sideways, as if to say, "Hello, friend."

TARRAGONA

by Diana Pullein-Thompson

Horse dealing in our childhood was a dicey business and none too honest. There weren't so many rules about fair trading in those days, and, at certain sales where rules were laid down, there was little comeback if you were done. You simply had to be careful and knowledgeable.

The horse dealer who had sold our parents an aged pony saying that she was seven years old used to bring us ponies to try out for him. We would keep them for a while, school them and ride them in local gymkhanas and he would bring his possible buyers to see them at our place. We made no charge for the schooling. We gained experience from it, and some of the ponies we could use later on for our pupils. If we managed to sell one of the dealer's animals for more than his asking price we were allowed to keep the change.

There was one pony called Tarragona, whom we particularly liked. She was fourteen one hands high, very dark bay with black points, with a head that was a little too long to be beautiful. Tarragona was wilful, intelligent and quite unstoppable, but she looked as though she could be turned into a good jumper. At the second show I rode her in she jumped me out of the ring over three rows of chairs, fortunately unoccupied at the time. Once, when I was riding her bareback in a headcollar through our village, she was frightened by white rags tied to barbed wire and took me for a John Gilpin ride at full gallop. I thundered past our house and stables, down a steep hill and across a main road, before another steep hill on the main bus route forced her to lessen her speed and I was able to turn her into a driveway.

On another occasion, when coming face to face with a lorry she didn't like on the Reading to Bath road, she leaped over a hedge and landed beside a row of tables in the garden of a café called The Wee Waif. The café's customers looked alarmed, but I had ridden her out again through the exit before they had time to say anything.

Yet, in spite of all her shortcomings, we liked Tarragona and we wanted her for ourselves and to use in the riding school, which was growing rapidly in size. But we could not, at that time, afford the twenty-five pounds which the dealer was asking for her.

As the days went by, Tarragona's mouth and manners improved. She quickly learned simple dressage movements and, although her action was not free enough to make us suppose that she would ever be top class, it was obvious that many riders could learn much from her. She had one failing, however, which no amount of schooling could cure.

It was a matter of temperament, something deep-rooted and unusual, which we found rather endearing. She could not bear people laughing in front of her. A smile was just bearable, but a laugh would turn her face ugly. In a trice she would lay back her ears and sink her teeth in the part of the laugher nearest to her. Of course, such eccentric behaviour could be dangerous, and although the tactics we used could be called dishonest, they were also protecting a possible buyer from landing himself with a biter whom he might not understand.

We were young most of our friends were still at school—and we were hard-up. There was an obvious way to reduce Tarragona's price, which we could justify by telling ourselves that she would be better with us where her particular weakness was well understood and not in any way resented. We informed our dealer that she was inclined to bite (which was part of but not the whole truth). He looked at us with his faded blue eyes set deep in a face the colour of tripe. A watch chain lay across his plump belly; his pale moustache twitched. His rather podgy hands came out of his pockets, where they had been jingling coins.

"As long as she won't hurt any kiddies . . ."

That was his rule. He would lie about the age of ponies, about their origins; he would put boot polish on a scar and keep quiet about a jibber. The unwary would pay him twice as much as a pony was worth if they weren't careful, and he wouldn't turn a hair. So long as he felt the pony was not dangerous for children to handle. Any animal he considered truly vicious would be sent by him to Reading Market to be auctioned without warranty.

"No, she might bite one, but she wouldn't kill it," we replied, very matter of fact and down to earth.

"We needn't mention it," he said.

And a few days later he brought middle-aged parents with a thirteen-year-old girl to see Tarragona. We didn't like them; they seemed dull and stodgy without sparkle, but we rode Tarragona as well as we could. The girl, we thought, was weak—a spineless child. She needed a more reliable pony.

"A fine little jumper," the dealer said, after we had popped Tarragona over a pair of hurdles. "A lovely pony that, a real winner."

The parents spoke little, seeming to communicate through glances at one another. The bun-faced girl showed no special enthusiasm. After a while we returned Tarragona to her loosebox, and then, as the parents leaned over the door to take another look at her, we laughed. In an instant her head came up; her ears flashed back and she bared her teeth. Her head, ugly in anger, shot over the door, and the prospective buyers leaped back only just in time.

"She would never have suited them. She would have been quite miserable with them and sooner or later she would have got the upper hand and started to run away with the girl," we told each other afterwards. And we were probably quite right.

And so a pattern was set. Each time a buyer came we laughed at some opportune moment when we were almost within reach of being bitten, although we always dodged away in the nick of time. The sight of those flattened ears, flashing teeth and sneering nostrils were guaranteed to send any possible purchaser home.

After a while our dealer friend began to despair a little. What could he do with her? He supposed we wouldn't want her by any chance? We offered him fifteen pounds, and he said he would let her go for twenty. He stood in our yard in his checked suit and laced boots, a shortish plump figure, a greengrocer who hadn't ridden himself for years, if at all. He wasn't fond of horses; they were simply part of trade, although he had a special love for coaches and carriages. Bargaining was part of that trade. It was the breath of life to him.

"Seventeen pounds," we said.

He agreed. We shook hands. He watched me write the cheque.

"Not like that," he said. "Never leave a gap there. Someone could put a one in front of seventeen and make it one hundred and seventeen. And don't leave a space there either or a sharp customer could add nineteen shillings."

Tarragona was the first pony we bought outright. The earlier ones had been paid for by instalments as we earned the money needed. We owned her for many years until we gave her away to a good home when she grew too old for riding school work. She won scores of prizes at local gymkhanas, first with me, and then with our cousin, Paulla, and various pupils. She helped all sorts of people to improve their jumping and learn elementary dressage. But we respected her sensitive feelings, her hatred of what she must have seen as ridicule. Laughing was banned when she was around, except once in a while when somebody could not believe that she lacked a sense of humour. Then her demonstration was fierce enough to settle the matter once and for all.

AN OLD-FASHIONED CURE

by James Herriott

As I stopped my car by the group of gipsies I felt I was looking at something which should have been captured by a camera. The grass verge was wide on this loop of the road and there were five of them squatting round the fire; it seemed like the mother and father and three little girls. They sat very still, regarding me blankly through the drifting smoke while a few big snowflakes floated across the scene and settled lazily on the tangled hair of the children. Some unreal quality in the wild tableau kept me motionless in my seat, staring through the glass, forgetful of the reason for my being here. Then I wound down the window and spoke to the man.

"Are you Mr. Myatt? I believe you have a sick pony." The man nodded. "Aye, that's right. He's over here." It was a strange accent with no trace of Yorkshire in it. He got up from the fire, a thin, dark-skinned unshaven little figure, and came over to the car holding out something in his hand. It was a ten shilling note and I recognised it as a gesture of good faith.

The gipsies who occasionally wandered into Darrowby were always regarded with a certain amount of suspicion. They came, unlike the Myatts, mainly in the summer to camp down by the river and sell their horses and we had been caught out once or twice before. A lot of them seemed to be called Smith and it wasn't uncommon to go back on the second day and find that patient and owner had gone. In fact Siegfried had shouted to me as I left the house this morning "Get the brass if you can." But he needn't have worried—Mr. Myatt was on the up and up.

I got out of the car and followed him over the grass, past the shabby, ornate caravan and the lurcher dog tied to the wheel to where a few horses and ponies were tethered. My patient was easy to find; a handsome piebald of about thirteen hands with good, clean legs and a look of class about him. But he was in a sorry state. While the other animals moved around on their tethers, watching us with interest, the piebald stood as though carved from stone.

Even from a distance I could tell what was wrong with him. Only acute laminitis could produce that crouching posture and as I moved nearer I could see that all four feet were probably affected because the pony had his hind feet right under his body in a desperate attempt to take his full weight on his heels.

I pushed my thermometer into the rectum. "Has he been getting any extra food, Mr. Myatt?"

"Aye, he getten into a bag of oats last night." The little man showed me the big, half empty sack in the back of the caravan. It was difficult to understand him but he managed to convey that the pony had broken loose and gorged himself on the oats.

And he had given him a dose of castor oil—he called it "casta ile".

The thermometer read 104 and the pulse was rapid and bounding. I passed my hand over the smooth, trembling hooves, feeling the abnormal heat, then I looked at the taut face, the dilated nostrils and terrified eyes. Anybody who has had an infection under a finger-nail can have an inkling of the agony a horse goes through when the sensitive laminae of the foot are inflamed and throbbing against the unyielding wall of the hoof.

"Can you get him to move?" I asked.

The man caught hold of the headcollar and pulled, but the pony refused to budge.

I took the other side of the collar. "Come on, it's always better if they can get moving."

We pulled together and Mrs. Myatt slapped the pony's rump. He took a couple of stumbling steps but it was as though the ground was red hot and he groaned as his feet came down. Within seconds he was crouching again with his weight on his heels.

"It seems he just won't have it." I turned and went back to the car. I'd have to do what I could to give him relief and the first thing was to get rid of as much as possible of that bellyful of oats. I fished out the bottle of arecoline and gave an injection into the muscle of the neck, then I showed the little man how to tie cloths round the hooves so that he could keep soaking them with cold water.

Afterwards I stood back and looked again at the pony. He was salivating freely from the arecoline and he had cocked his tail and evacuated his bowel; but his pain was undiminished and it would stay like that until the tremendous inflammation subsided—if it ever did. I had seen cases like this where serum had started to ooze from the coronet; that usually meant shedding of the hooves—even death.

As I turned over these gloomy thoughts the three little girls went up to the pony. The biggest put her arms round his neck and laid her cheek against his shoulder while the others stroked the shivering flanks. There were no tears, no change in the blank expressions, but it was easy to see that that pony really meant something to them.

Before leaving I handed over a bottle of tincture of aconite mixture. "Get a dose of this down him every four hours, Mr. Myatt, and be sure to keep putting cold water on the feet. I'll come and see him in the morning."

I closed the car door and looked through the window again at the slow-rising smoke, the drifting snowflakes and the three children with their ragged dresses and uncombed hair still stroking the pony.

"Well, you got the brass, James," Siegfried said at lunch, carelessly stuffing the ten shilling note into a bulging pocket. "What was the trouble?"

"Worst case of laminitis I've ever seen. Couldn't move the pony at all, and he's going through hell. I've done the usual things but I'm pretty sure they aren't going to be enough."

"Not a very bright prognosis, then?"

"Really black. Even if he gets over the acute stage

he'll have deformed feet, I'd like to bet. Grooved hooves, dropped soles, the lot. And he's a grand little animal, lovely piebald. I wish to God there was something else I could do."

Siegfried sawed two thick slices off the cold mutton and dropped them on my plate. He looked thoughtfully at me for a moment. "You've been a little distrait since you came back. These are rotten jobs, I know, but it's no good worrying."

"Ach, I'm not worrying, exactly, but I can't get it off my mind. Maybe it's those people—the Myatts. They were something new to me. Right out of the world. And three raggedy little girls absolutely crazy about that pony. They aren't going to like it at all."

As Siegfried chewed his mutton I could see the old glint coming into his eyes; it showed when the talk had anything to do with horses. I knew he wouldn't push in but he was waiting for me to make the first move. I made it.

"I wish you'd come along and have a look with me. Maybe there's something you could suggest. Do you think there could be?"

Siegfried put down his knife and fork and stared in front of him for a few seconds, then he turned to me. "You know, James, there just might be. Quite obviously this is a right pig of a case and the ordinary remedies aren't going to do any good. We have to pull something out of the bag and I've got an idea. There's just one thing." He gave me a crooked smile. "You may not like it."

"Don't bother about me," I said. "You're the horseman. If you can help this pony I don't care what you do."

"Right, eat up then and we'll go into action together." We finished our meal and he led me through to the instrument room. I was surprised when he opened the cupboard where old Mr. Grant's instruments were kept. It was a kind of museum.

When Siegfried had bought the practice from the old vet who had worked on into his eighties these instruments had come with it and they lay there in rows, unused but undisturbed. It would have been logical to throw them out, but maybe Siegfried felt the same way about them as I did. The polished wooden boxes of shining, odd-shaped scalpels, the enema pumps and douches with their perished rubber and brass fittings, the seaton needles, the ancient firing irons—they were a silent testament to sixty years of struggle. I often used to open the cupboard door and try to picture the old man wrestling with the same problems as I had, travelling the same narrow roads as I did. He had done it absolutely on his own and for sixty years. I was only starting but I knew a little about the triumphs and disappointments—and the hard labour. Anyway, Mr. Grant was dead and gone, taking with him all the skills and knowledge I was doggedly trying to accumulate.

Siegfried reached to the back of the cupboard and pulled out a long flat box. He blew the dust from the leather covering and gingerly unfastened the clasp. Inside, a fleam, glittering on its bed of frayed velvet, lay by the side of a round, polished blood stick.

I looked at my employer in astonishment. "You're going to bleed him, then?"

"Yes, my boy, I'm going to take you back to the Middle Ages." He looked at my startled face and put a hand on my arm. "But don't start beating me over the head with all the scientific arguments against blood-letting. I've no strong views either way."

"But have you ever done it? I've never seen you use this outfit."

"I've done it. And I've seen some funny things after it, too." Siegfried turned away as if he wanted no more discussion. He cleaned the fleam thoroughly and dropped it into the steriliser. His face was expressionless as he stood listening to the hiss of the boiling water.

The gipsies were again hunched over the fire when we got there and Mr. Myatt, sensing that reinforcements had arrived, scrambled to his feet and shuffled forward, holding out another ten shilling note.

Siegfried waved it away. "Let's see how we get on, Mr. Myatt," he grunted. He strode across the grass to where the pony still trembled in his agonized crouch. There was no improvement; in fact the eyes stared more wildly and I could hear little groans as the piebald carefully eased himself from foot to foot.

Siegfried spoke softly without looking at me, "Poor beggar. You weren't exaggerating, James. Bring that box from the car, will you?"

When I came back he was tying a choke rope round the base of the pony's neck. "Pull it up tight," he said. As the jugular rose up tense and turgid in its furrow he quickly clipped and disinfected a small area and inserted a plaque of local anaesthetic. Finally he opened the old leather-covered box and extracted the fleam, wrapped in sterile lint.

Everything seemed to start happening then. Siegfried placed the little blade of the fleam against the bulging vein and without hesitation gave it a confident smack with the stick. Immediately an alarming cascade of blood spouted from the hole and began to form a dark lake on the grass. Mr. Myatt gasped and the little girls set up a sudden chatter. I could understand how they felt. In fact I was wondering how long the pony could stand this tremendous outflow without dropping down.

It didn't seem to be coming out fast enough for Siegfried, however, because he produced another stick from his pocket, thrust it into the pony's mouth and began to work the jaws. And as the animal champed, the blood gushed more fiercely.

When at least a gallon had come away Siegfried seemed satisfied. "Slacken the rope, James," he cried, then rapidly closed the wound on the neck with a pin suture. Next he trotted over the grass and looked over a gate in the roadside wall. "Thought so," he shouted. "There's a little beck in that field. We've got to get him over to it. Come on, lend a hand everybody!"

He was clearly enjoying himself and his presence was having its usual effect. The Myatts were spurred suddenly into action and began to run around aimlessly, bumping into each other. I was gripped by a sudden tension and preparedness and even the pony seemed to be taking an interest in his surroundings for the first time.

All five of the gipsies pulled at the halter, Siegfried and I looped our arms behind the pony's thighs, everybody gave encouraging shouts and at last he began to move forward. It was a painful process but he kept going—through the gate and across the field to where the shallow stream wandered among its rushes. There were no banks to speak of and it was easy to push him out into the middle. As he stood there with the icy water rippling round his inflamed hooves I fancied I could read in his eyes a faint dawning of an idea that things were looking up at last.

"Now he must stand in there for an hour," Siegfried said. "And then you'll have to make him walk round the field. Then another hour in the beck. As he gets better you can give him more and more exercise but he must come back to the beck. There's a lot of work for somebody here, so who's going to do it?"

The three little girls came shyly round him and looked up, wide-eyed, into his face. Siegfried laughed. "You three want the job, do you? Right, I'll tell you just what to do."

He pulled out the bag of peppermint drops which was ever-present among his widely-varied pocket luggage and I settled myself for a long wait. I had seen him in action with the children on the farms and when that bag of sweets came out, everything stopped. It was the one time Siegfried was never in a hurry.

The little girls each solemnly took a sweet, then

Siegfried squatted on his heels and began to address them like a professor with his class. They soon began to thaw and put a word in for themselves. The smallest launched into a barely intelligible account of the remarkable things the pony had done when he was a foal and Siegfried listened intently, nodding his head gravely now and then. There was all the time in the world.

His words obviously went home because, over the next few days whenever I passed the gipsy camp I could see the three wild little figures either grouped around the pony in the beck or dragging him round the field on a long halter shank. I didn't need to butt in—I could see he was improving all the time.

It was about a week later that I saw the Myatts on their way out of Darrowby, the red caravan rocking across the market place with Mr. Myatt up front wearing a black velvet cap, his wife by his side. Tethered to various parts of the caravan the family of horses clopped along and right at the rear was the piebald, a bit stiff perhaps, but going very well. He'd be all right.

The little girls were looking out of the back door and as they spotted me I waved. They looked back at me unsmilingly until they had almost turned the corner into Hallgate then one of them shyly lifted her hand. The others followed suit and my last sight was of them waving eagerly back.

I strolled into the Drovers and took a thoughtful half pint into a corner. Siegfried had done the trick there all right but I was wondering what to make of it because in veterinary practice it is difficult to draw definite conclusions even after spectacular results. Was it my imagination or did that pony seem to feel relief almost immediately after the blood-letting? Would we ever have got him moving without it? Was it really the right thing in these cases to bash a hole in the jugular and release about a bucketful of the precious fluid? I still don't have the answers because I never dared try it for myself.

RESCUE AT TEA-TIME

by Christine Pullein-Thompson

It was tea-time when the telephone rang. I picked up the receiver and a woman's voice said, "There's a mad boy on a mad horse in my garden and they're trampling on everything. The police are here, but they won't do a thing. Will you come and remove them?"

I knew her name and where she lived, but we had never met. I had no idea how she knew me. Still, it was a challenging situation and I thought perhaps I could help, so I said, "O.K., I'll be along in a few minutes," and rang off.

I put on my mackintosh with large pockets and filled them with pony nuts. I fetched a halter and half a bucketful of oats and jumped into my ancient Austin Cambridge car. The house was less than a mile away and when I reached it there were Panda cars outside and policemen with checked bands on their caps standing about. One of them looked at me and said, "We can't get the boy off, and we're not allowed to touch the horse without his permission."

The horse was a large bay mare steaming with sweat. At intervals she let out a wild mustang-like snort, and I could see sheep nearby huddled against a fence. The boy was young, about fifteen, and wore no hat. They were in an orchard and the mare was rearing, and each time she went up on her hind legs, the boy's face disappeared among apple branches, to re-emerge even more bloodstained than it was before. He was repeating over and over again like a robot, the strange words, "This horse is nappy. It must go forward."

I had never seen either of them before and there was no sign of the lady who had telephoned.

"We can't do a thing with the boy," said one of the policemen.

They were very tall men. I am five feet five, but I felt a dwarf beside them. I walked into the orchard and started to shout at the boy, "She isn't nappy! She's afraid of the sheep. Get off *at once*." I was sure he was concussed and I have been concussed myself, so I knew how he was feeling (I too had talked like a robot). And on such occasions you have to give orders rather than make polite requests. He started to swear at me and I yelled back, "*Get off at once*!" in the voice our old family nurse had used to me years ago. And somehow, miraculously, it worked. He got off, shouting more oaths, while I grabbed the sweating, plunging mare, certain that once she had left the sheep she would be all right. The police took the boy into the house. I led the mare away, talking to her, feeling the tension go out of her.

Some of the police followed me home driving my old car. They told me I was brave—which wasn't true, I just knew about horses and they didn't. I stood for ages calming the mare, giving her grass.

The lady of the house never appeared and has never thanked me for saving her garden from further damage. Later I led the mare, riding one of our ponies, back to the stables where she lived. Riding Airborne home in the dusk, I pondered how the boy and the horse had ever reached the garden and the sheep. And how did the boy get concussed without falling off? Or had he taken a toss and remounted?

It was several days later before I was able to put the whole story together as far as it will ever be known. The boy couldn't tell us anything, because when you're concussed you can't remember anything which happened just before the accident, and for some time afterwards—it is just a blank. But it seems he was a working pupil at the stables and, since no one wanted to ride the bay mare, he offered to take her out alone. He knew she was difficult, but he was willing to have a go.

All went well until he reached the common beyond the yard gate; then she reared and set off like a bolt from the blue, and when she reared her head met the boy's head. How far they galloped will never be known, but the blow must have caused instant concussion for from then on he was only partly conscious of what was happening, like a sleep walker—except that he was riding instead of walking. He must have ridden four or five miles like this and then suddenly seen the main road ahead, and turned into the garden to be confronted by the sheep. The mare was obviously nappy, or so he had been told, and nappy horses and rearers should be driven forward, hence the words "It must go forward."

Of course, a working pupil should never be allowed to go out on a difficult horse alone; nor should anyone ride without a hard hat (which incidentally would have protected his head and saved him from concussion). Luckily the boy soon recovered, and the horse was removed from the stables by her owner. Personally, I think she had a sore or a fistulous wither, but that's another story . . .

THE NATIONAL HERO

by Michael Hardcastle

On summer evenings boats filled with passengers would glide along the Leeds–Liverpool Canal. The guide on these pleasure cruises would point out places of interest and one or two people would nod appreciatively and the occasional camera would click. Then, as they approached a three-acre paddock beside the waterway, the guide announced: "And now, on your left, you can see the most famous racehorse in Britain."

No one had to be told that this was Red Rum. everyone wanted to see him and every camera was trained on him. Red Rum, thoroughly enjoying his summer holiday and romping around the field with Andy the donkey, didn't mind at all. He's used to crowds and cameras and constant admiration.

Yet, only a few weeks earlier, in the spring of 1975, the ten-year-old bay gelding had been beaten into second place in the Grand National, the world's greatest steeplechase. For the first time in three years Red Rum wasn't the winner. He had been carrying top weight of twelve stone and the ground was softer than Red Rum likes it.

"It was his courage which got him to the last fence

that day," says his trainer, Donald 'Ginger' McCain. "Red Rum doesn't recognise defeat."

Nor do his devoted fans. Weeks afterwards they were still sending him presents or calling to see him in his box in the stables behind a car showroom in Southport, near Liverpool. Letters and telegrams came pouring in from all parts of the world, from America and Australia and New Zealand and even from the captain and crew of a ship in the middle of the Indian Ocean. Polo mints and postal orders (to buy more sweets) and even a shawl from an old lady arrived for him. People on holiday in the seaside town turned up to see him at the rate of sixty a week and wanted to stay so long that they were holding up the work in the stables.

Most of the letter-writers were greatly upset about the result of the 1975 Grand National and they were sending their heartfelt sympathy.

One young girl wrote: "Don't worry, Red Rum, you're *still* the greatest!"

And so he is. For his achievements on the racecourse may never be beaten. Few horses have won two Grand Nationals in successive years and none has won in a faster time than Red Rum's in 1973. The following year he became the first horse ever to win the Liverpool race and the Scottish Grand National at Ayr in the same season. He is the only horse to have his statue put up on a racecourse in his lifetime.

Red Rum has inspired so much devotion not only because of his marvellous performances as a steeplechaser. He is loved by countless people who know hardly anything about racing simply because of his character and courage.

He wasn't bred to jump fences, or even to run in long distance races. His parents were sprinters. Foaled in County Kilkenny, Southern Ireland, on May 3rd, 1965, he was the third offspring, and first son, of a mare called Mared, who had the reputation of being a bit mad. His sire was a grey, Quorum, who'd been a very fast horse in his day. Because many racehorses are named fairly directly after their parents, the bay colt by Quorum out of Mared might well have been called Rum Red, but as it turned out his first English owner reversed those names.

Horses intended for a career as steeplechasers often don't even see a racecourse until they are aged four or five. But Red Rum was bought at an auction, for four hundred guineas, to go racing even before he was two years old. From Ireland he went to Leicestershire and into the care of Tim Molony, a former champion steeplechase jockey who is now a trainer. His job was to prepare Red Rum for a small race at Liverpool on the day before the 1967 Grand National.

It is one of the many coincidences in the life of Red Rum that he should start his racing career on the course where he was to have his greatest triumphs. Liverpool does not have many flat races nowadays and the one in which Red Rum ran that day was the very poorest kind of race; the Grand National is the richest steeplechase of all in Britain. His first race was run over a distance of five furlongs; the National is almost exactly four miles longer.

He won it—but only just, for it was in the very last stride that he caught the leader, a filly called Curlicue, and forced a dead-heat. Slowly away from the start, he'd been ridden strongly to make a race of it and share the prize (which amounted to £133 for his owner). A hard race like that may have a lasting effect on some horses but Red Rum was to prove that he didn't resent his introduction to racing.

It was a condition of the race he'd won that the winner had to be offered for sale immediately but no one outbid Mr. Molony, and so Red Rum returned to the stables in Leicestershire. Much later on that season Red Rum won again—by a neck, at Warwick—and among the jockeys who rode him was Lester Piggott. In all, he ran eight times, from April to September, as a two-year-old. He was learning about life as a racehorse the hard way.

As soon as the next flat racing season opened Red Rum was in action again—and again a 'selling' race was his objective. This was to be over seven furlongs at Doncaster and he won it by a very narrow margin, a head. This time he was 'sold' on Mr. Molony's final bid for 1,400 guineas—and three days later Red Rum was racing again. He was taken back to Liverpool on another Grand National day and, with Lester Piggott in the saddle, he finished second, beaten by only a short head, in a handicap over a mile. As it turned out, it was to be Red Rum's last race on the flat.

Meanwhile, that same afternoon in March, 1968, the Grand National was being won by a horse called Red Alligator, ridden by Brian Fletcher—the jockey who, five years later, was to win the great race on another 'Red'.

Three times in less than three years Red Rum had been offered for sale at a public auction but when he changed hands again shortly after that Liverpool race the deal was arranged privately. His new owner was a lady who lived in Yorkshire; she had won the Grand National with a horse called Freebooter in 1950 and she wanted to win it again. So Red Rum went to her trainer in Ripon to be prepared for racing 'over the jumps'.

For four years he remained in Yorkshire, winning eight races over hurdles and fences on a variety of courses. Then it was discovered that he had a disease of the foot in his off-fore, a condition rather like arthritis in humans. It made it painful for him to walk, let alone run, and at one stage it seemed possible that he might never race again. But from his stable-girl Red Rum received tender and loving care and he began to recover.

It was in the summer of 1972 that he was sold again—for six thousand guineas this time—and the man who bought him had been wanting to win the Grand National for more than sixty years. It was the one unfulfilled ambition of his long life and he had spent more than £100,000 in trying to make his dream come true. His name is Noel Le Mare, and it's another of those extraordinary coincidences in Red Rum's life that his dam is called Mared.

In 1906, Noel Le Mare, already becoming fascinated by the Grand National, was a teenager working on trawlers. In Fleetwood one day he watched in wonderment as an American visitor handed out gold sovereigns as gifts. Young Noel vowed then that he himself would become a millionaire, would marry a beautiful woman and would lead a Grand National runner into the winner's enclosure as its owner. He achieved his first two ambitions.

Then, in 1959, a horse of his won a hurdle race at Liverpool and Mr. Le Mare made a foolish declaration. "I said that if my wish to win the National came true then the Lord could take me." Five years later, as he watched his National runner in the parade ring, he suddenly thought: "Oh, no. If this wins I've got to go! So I told my chauffeur, Joe, ring up God and tell him I've ratted on my promise!" The horse didn't win.

That was the story Mr. Le Mare told me before the 1973 Grand National and he was to tell it to others umpteen times after that race. After all, it fits in perfectly among the other amazing legends associated with Grand National winners.

Southport is only a dozen miles from Aintree, Liverpool's racecourse. Southport is where Mr. Le Mare lives and where Red Rum was to be trained by 'Ginger' McCain, a man to whom the National had meant so much that he became engaged on the day of one Grand National and married on another. Now he has other reasons as well for remembering for the rest of his life the world's most exciting steeplechase.

'Ginger' is a genial man, helpful and friendly, and his beaming smile hides the hard times he experienced before Red Rum entered his life. He had trained horses for several years without much success and it was his second-hand car business that kept him going as a trainer. He also ran a taxi business and when, one evening, he drove Mr. Le Mare to a local hotel they began to talk about horses—and the Grand National . . .

His stables are in what was once a brewery yard, close to a railway track in an ordinary suburb. So, for his gallops, the trainer has always used the beach which is only a little over a mile away from the stables. Bordered by high dunes, it's a wide and sandy beach—so wide, in fact, that it's the only one in the country to be used regularly in summer as an airfield.

The salt water and the soft sand were exactly the tonic that Red Rum needed. Without doubt, they helped enormously to restore him to full strength and health. The beach and the dunes and the sea were his playground as well as the place where he trained for his races.

His first race in the colours of his new owner (maroon with a yellow diamond) was at Carlisle and he was ridden by Tommy Stack, a man who had briefly been one of his trainers in Yorkshire and who was to ride him in the 1976 Grand National. Tommy was frankly amazed at the difference in Red Rum's performance and well-being. That was the first of five successive victories for Red Rum. He was approaching his peak—and he reached it at Aintree, displaying yet again his astonishing courage and determination.

Red Rum has always revelled in fast going (a firm racing surface) and the sun on his back; in spring his exuberance matches the name of the season and, bucking and kicking and frolicking, he can be hard to hold in the paddock before the start of a race. Yet he wasn't at all disturbed by the BBC Television cameras that whirred away in his box on the morning of his first National. Like so many great horses, he's intelligent, and the extra fuss being made of him that day was something to be enjoyed. In Yorkshire he used to kick out at passing cars, but since moving to Lancashire traffic no longer bothered him; so the fairground atmosphere of Aintree on 'National' day certainly wasn't going to worry him.

The sun was shining that afternoon of the last day of March. 'Ginger' McCain had been very candid about his horse's chances of winning the great race and Red Rum had captured the public's imagination. He became joint-favourite at 9–1 with Crisp, an Australian horse who was carrying top weight of twelve stone. There were thirty-six other runners, thirty huge fences to be jumped and four miles and eight hundred and fifty-six yards to be covered.

Crisp soon blazed into the lead, jumping quite magnificently and setting a cracking pace. Some of the runners did crack but Red Rum's jockey, Brian

Fletcher, was faithfully following his plan to make steady progress on the first circuit and avoid trouble. Leaping like a stag, Crisp was twenty lengths in front at Becher's the second time round but by now Red Rum was in second place and jumping equally as well, if not so spectacularly. At the last fence Crisp was still more than ten lengths ahead but his big weight was taking its toll of even his strength.

The long run-in from the final fence to the winning post at Aintree has been the scene of some epic struggles between valiant horses. Now the crowd was witnessing another as Crisp, tiring rapidly, wandered off a straight line and Red Rum relentlessly closed the gap separating them. At the post the winner was Red Rum, by just three-quarters of a length. For the first time for several minutes spectators could breathe freely again and mop their brows. No one was surprised that the time for the race was a record: Red Rum had won in a fraction over nine minutes and lopped nearly twenty seconds off the previous fastest time. He was, as someone said, "indomitable". There can't be a better description of his performance.

Many National winners never again face the massive Aintree obstacles and some are quickly retired from all racing. Yet, after a summer's rest, Red Rum was soon in action again—and back in the winner's enclosure. He won four times more before returning to Liverpool the following spring to attempt a feat that hadn't been accomplished for almost forty years: winning the National twice in succession. This time Crisp wasn't in the race and it was Red Rum now who had top weight of twelve stone. Some thought that would stop him and a horse called Scout was made favourite.

'Ginger' McCain had confidently been predicting victory and then, on the night before the race: "I suddenly thought, he has forty-one to beat, he's carrying top weight and who knows what will happen in that race. I was too cocky and I admit it. It's easy for me to sit in a chair and predict: Red Rum has to go and do it."

As it turned out, 'Ginger', who's as honest as his hero, had no cause to worry. For Red Rum made it look almost incredibly easy. Eager to get on with things, he took over the lead at Becher's the second time round and eventually won by seven lengths. At the finish he appeared to be going as strongly as ever. Spelt backwards, Red Rum is 'murder'—and, in racing terms, he had certainly murdered his distinguished opponents.

For his delighted owner Red Rum had proved that *some* dreams do come true, even twice over! In spite of that promise he'd 'ratted on' many years earlier, Mr. Le Mare was still very much in the land of the living and Red Rum had now won him over £50,000 in those two Grand Nationals. Three weeks later the old gentleman collected another £8,000 when 'Rummy' turned out for the Scottish Grand National and, a hot favourite, won that, too. No wonder Ayr management put up a statue to him on the course itself.

It was after his second National success at Liverpool that a Sussex lady wrote to a sporting paper to say she was horrified to learn that his Sunday visitors had fed him ninety-six packets of mints and endless carrots. "It is obvious that Red Rum has an iron constitution," she added. But she didn't think all those tit-bits could be good for him. Red Rum continued to chomp away happily. He has always had a huge appetite and there's nothing finicky about it, either. His dislikes are restricted to having his coat clipped and being 'plated' (having his racing shoes put on).

Naturally, as he has grown older, his speed has diminished, though his stamina seems as great as ever. He has jumped more than 1,000 fences on courses all over Britain without falling once, for he has a cat-like ability to sidestep danger. In spite of all the hard knocks he's taken in his life, on and off the racecourse, he has never flinched from any task he's been given. His determination to do his best always and his courage are boundless. His heart is as big as any fence he's jumped.

When, in 1975, he went back to Liverpool to try for a record-breaking third success the ground was softer than he likes it. The weight he had to give to L'Escargot proved too much and Red Rum finished second. In 1976 he was second again, though beaten by only two lengths by Rag Trade—and he was running on again tigerishly at the finish. On both occasions he'd been beaten by top-class horses: L'Escargot had twice won the Cheltenham Gold Cup while Rag Trade had previously won two minor Nationals, the Welsh and Midland.

So, in seven races at Liverpool, on the flat and over

hurdles and fences, and including four successive Grand Nationals, Red Rum has never finished out of the first two places. It is an achievement that surely will never be equalled.

Deservedly, it has made him the National hero.

A RIDE BY THE SEA

by Monica Dickens

I am going alone, with John in the trailer, to ride on Sandy Neck, a seven mile sandbar between the ocean and the great marsh on the other side of Cape Cod from where I live.

It is a day at the end of summer, with a deep blue September sky. The maples and locust trees are just beginning to hint at the golds and oranges and flaring autumn reds that will send people driving all over New England, taking photographs and crying, "Will you look at that *colour*!"

You can only ride on Sandy Neck before the summer tourists have come, or after they have gone home to put their children back into school. The parking place is deserted except for the few cars of people surf fishing or walking on the dunes and the long curving beach, and one or two mad characters swimming in the icy waters of Cape Cod Bay.

John backs neatly out of the trailer, and after a small amount of difficulty with the saddle and bridle, because the ocean wind excites him, we start off with the dog Charlie along the wide marsh at the back of the dunes.

John flexes his black neck and steps out at once,

two of his chronic coughs, then a series of healthy snorts to clear out his pipes. John is a quarter horse, just over fifteen hands, short-backed and springy, handily supple, with the pigeon toes of his breed and a rather thick neck disguised by his full glossy mane. This neck is so crested that when I bought him, with a stiff untrimmed hogged mane, he looked like a Greek horse on the frieze of the Parthenon.

The sand track round the marsh is soft in places, in others hard enough to trot and canter. Gulls and marsh birds rise from the wet land as we come round corners, following the curves of the dunes. In a patch of salty grass and stunted trees, all blowing away from the sea, a small fox gets up, and Charlie goes after it, yelping, but not catching it, although it runs quite slowly, and even stops on a rise and turns to look for him.

Half a dozen tiny cabins sit with their backs to the sand dunes, their rickety porches looking out over the wide green marsh. With no road, no water or electricity, no heat except the fires of driftwood they collect, some people live here until well into winter before they return unwillingly to civilization.

In a grey weathered shack all hung about with the coloured floats and glass balls and lobster pots that the sea has brought him, a man sits by a window. He has a beard and a thick pullover and a pipe, and a typewriter on the table.

We wave as I trot past, and I think we envy each other. He would like to be me out here in the sun and wind, instead of chained to a typewriter indoors. I would like to be writing there in such peace and stillness. What a place to write a book!

And yet, if one had all that beauty beyond the window, the birds and the changing colours of the marsh and its imperceptibly changing shapes as the tide seeps in and out, one might be too busy watching to write a line. If you want to write, it's better to shut yourself into a tiny room with a blank wall in front of you. Perhaps the beard and the pipe and the typewriter are disguises to make the man feel like a writer. Perhaps he isn't writing at all.

A sand hill hides his cottage from the sight of John stopping dead, and pitching me forward on his neck. Thanks for keeping your head up. Where streams under the dunes surface and run into the marsh, there are plank bridges, just two boards with a hole full of water between. A horse can't walk over them. John fusses and tramples a bit, finally jumps the bridge and stream quite neatly, and jumps the next one and the next and the next with less and less fuss. If we were going the other way, towards home, he would not fuss at any of them.

At the end of the broad spit of sand where the marsh opens out into the sea at Barnstable, we turn across the dunes towards the beach. The path runs through a struggling grove of flat-topped firs like a Japanese print, growing out of nothing but sand. One of the underground streams runs near the surface here. Charlie stops to dig, tail in the air, leaning on the elbows to lick at the fresh water which seeps through the dark sand where his paws have scrabbled.

Through a cut in the last steeper rise of barrier dune, with the sand blowing off the top of it into our faces, and suddenly it is a clean wind blowing as we come through the gap—and behold the sea!

It's low tide. Mile after mile, the hard wet sand stretches away on either side of us into the shimmer of distance, and before us over the rippled beach shining with pools to where the low breakers fall.

We turn towards the lighthouse at the far end of the beach, a fast canter splattering the wet sand, jumping rivulets, swerving round shallow pools. Then we turn and let go—you can gallop for ever on this beach.

Going so fast, lowering his back, streamlining his ears, his salty mane blowing into my face, John doesn't jump the streams and swerve round the pools. He gallops right through them, splat, spatter, splat, and on to the hard sand again, both of us soaking wet, flying along the path of the sea wind.

. . . My horse a thing of wings, myself a god.

I let John gallop until he stops. There is no one on this beach but us. Far away, distorted by distance so that they seem to be hovering above the sand, a mirage of other horsemen is going towards or away from us.

We turn down to the sea, where Charlie has already

splashed out, barking at a seagull. I take off John's saddle, and take the rein off one side of the bit, to have a longer rein to hold him with. He paws at the surf with his neck arched, blowing the froth off it like beer and splashing his stomach. Then he sags and goes down. He flounders on one side, gets up and goes down on the other side, his thick tail lashing the water. Then he plunges out and goes down in the sand about half a dozen times. He can't get enough of this. He pulls back into the sea once more, then down on the beach to cover himself with the delicious gritty sand.

We walk up to where there is some coarse dune grass to eat, and idle in the sun till he is dry enough to brush the sand off his back and put on the saddle. Normally, he stands like a rock for me to get on, but now he turns as soon as my leg is over the saddle and we are off again across the drum-hard sand to the edge of the tide.

He slows to splash through an inlet to a long sandbar. At the far end of it, a dark mound like a rock becomes, as we canter closer, the body of a huge porpoise. John steps wide round it, snorting. Charlie, who likes to roll on dead things, can't find a place to start on this humped hulk, so he lifts his leg on it to show that he was there.

The sandbar runs diagonally back into the beach, and we cut up through the softer sand under the dunes, so as not to get mixed up with fishing lines. Beyond the ramp to the car park, a line of small cottages with steep roofs like Dutch houses sits along the dunes. I ride on a bit farther, so as to be able to jump the breakwater, jump it back again—John going very fast, with his head down like a bull—and turn up between the cottages to ride back through the dunes to the trailer.

The sun is lowering. A woman in a flowered hair net and mauve slacks faces the slanting warmth in a long chair on the deck of her little shingled house, which has hearts carved in the window shutters, and is labelled Crow's Nest. As I climb the sandy path at the side, I hope she will open her eyes, because it will be nice for her to see something so picturesque as John and me, fresh from our long gallop in the sea wind. If I was basking on the deck of Crow's Nest, I would love to see a nice-looking horse come by.

She does open her eyes. She lets go a cry of outrage and jumps to her feet. The mauve slacks are short and tight, with little bulges at the knees like cricket balls.

"Get off my land!"

I pull John up. "I thought——"

"That's the trouble with you people. You think you own it all."

"I thought it was a path to the beach."

"It's *my* path, and this is *my* house, and this is *my* bit of beach down to high tide mark."

"Can I go through now that I've come this far?"

"No."

"I'm not doing any harm. Surely a horse——"

"I hate 'em."

My horse a thing of wings, myself a god!

Unwillingly, as I turn back to the beach to find another way through, I recognise the astonishing truth that there are people who actually don't *like* to see a horse go by.

In the car park, I unsaddled John and put on his halter. Usually I can lead him straight into the trailer, but sometimes he will back straight out again, unless there is another person to snap the chain behind him.

This is one of those days. There is no reason. Three times John walks in. Three times he backs out again before I can get the chain up. You can't tie a horse in a trailer before he is shut in behind, because if he pulls back, and then gets frenzied, as horses do when they start pulling back, he'll break his halter at least, if not his neck. When I'm alone, I hang a bucket of oats up front to keep John busy while I slip back to fasten the chain. Today I have forgotten the oats, and the hay net doesn't interest him.

There is a red sports car parked, but no one about. At last, as John is clattering stupidly backwards for the fifth time (Don't you *want* to go home?), another car pulls up alongside.

I ask the driver for help. "Could you possibly stand behind him and fasten the chain while I——"

It is the woman in the hair net and mauve slacks. She has followed us to make sure we leave.

"——while I lead him in?"

She rolls up the window and turns on her radio.

The sun has gone down now behind the hills. The wind that blows across the marshes from the sea has a cold edge to it. The fishermen have gone. So have the people walking dogs. Except one. Far below on the beach, a small girl throws a stick for a big leaping dog. As I watch, a man's head comes over the edge of the dune. He climbs up and goes towards the red car.

When I ask him if he can help me, he is willing, but nervous.

"I don't know anything about horses."

"If you could just fasten the chain behind him."

"He'll kick me."

"No, he won't."

"I'm scared of both ends, but the back end is worse than the front."

"You lead him in then."

"He wouldn't come with me."

"He would."

"In *there*?" he peers into the trailer. He is a very nervous man, worry lines crumpling over a twitching eyebrow. "He'll tread on me."

"No, he won't."

"He'll run me down."

"You stand behind him then."

"He'll kick me."

We are back to where we started, when the child and the dog come panting over the top of the dune.

"She'll help you." The man's face uncrumples with relief.

Chewing her long salty hair, the little girl, who is about seven, takes John's halter rope, clucks to him, and with the confidence of an old groom, leads him into the trailer. I snap the chain, and he doesn't even lean backwards to see if it is there, but at once begins to bully the hay net like a boxer's punch bag.

The woman from Crow's Nest has of course driven away before she can witness our triumph. The father helps me to put up the tailgate. The child leans out of the small trailer door to ask which way I'm going. "I'll stay in here with him till where we turn off."

It is illegal for people to ride in horse trailers, but she has shut the door, so I drive off, the red car following, with the big dog sitting like a person in the front seat.

At the crossroads, the child hops out and squeezes into the red car beside the dog. He is bigger than she is. She doesn't wave or smile as they drive away. Her face is still absorbed with John.